UNDERSTANDING BUSIN

BUSINESS LAW

MADE EASY

Rob Dransfield

Published in 2003 by:
Nelson Thornes Ltd
Delta Place
27 Bath Road
CHELTENHAM
GL53 7TH
United Kingdom

A catalogue record for this book is available from the British
Library

ISBN 0 7487 6677 4

03 04 05 06 07 / 10 9 8 7 6 5 4 3 2 1

Illustrations by GreenGate Publishing Services and Alex Machin

Page make-up by GreenGate Publishing Services, Tonbridge, Kent

Printed and bound in Great Britain by Scotprint

The author would like to thank the library staff at Nottingham Trent
University for making available up-to-date journals and articles to
help in collecting information for this book. The author would also
like to thank his editor, Carolyn Lee, for the guidance and support
she has provided.

Thanks are due to the following for permission to use material
reproduced in this book:

The Court of Justice of the European Communities p.11,
Bettmann/Corbis p.79, Marks and Spencer p.25, Oxfam p.27,
Sainsbury's p.25, War Child p.25, Adam Woolfitt/Corbis p.3.

346.07

Contents

Unit 5: Consumer Protection Legislation

Unit 6: Employment Law

Preface

Doctor Proctor – your friendly guide to the world of Business Law.

Business Law is a popular option for many students, providing them with an important understanding of the legal framework in which businesses operate. The law acts as a constraint on the activities of a business, but it is also an enabler that protects the business from a range of harmful practices.

This book provides you with a good introductory guide to the various legal frameworks and laws that affect a business and is intended for students studying Advanced Level courses in business including the baccalaureate. Laws that are relevant to business include contract, employment, environment protection and consumer protection laws. The book also covers the legal implications of the types of business ownership, and an important theme is the growing importance of the European Union as a source of legislation.

This work breaks up key sections of the law into bitesize chunks to enable students to quickly develop an understanding of key points. Doctor Proctor is your friendly guide who sets out the material in a clear and easy to understand way to give you confidence as you build up an understanding of business law.

Typically legal documents are very wordy and take extensive reading by the legal specialist. Here we are more concerned with providing a good understanding to the business generalist who must know about the major framework of the laws which concern business. As a result Doctor Proctor provides legal explanations which are accessible to the typical student. He never seeks to confuse you by using unnecessary legal terminology. However, legal terms and descriptions are used when it is appropriate to give you a genuine introduction to legal ways of thinking at this level.

About the author

Rob Dransfield designs, leads and teaches on a number of Business related degrees at The Nottingham Trent University. His particular concern is to make business subjects accessible and interesting to all students.

How to use this book

As you work through the text, you'll find the following features to help you.

Key Ideas
These are some of the fundamental ideas on which Business Law is based.

You Must Know This
Terms and principles that you need to learn by heart and understand.

Dr Proctor says:
'You Must Know This!'

We use the term 'sources of law' to describe – where laws come from, i.e. who makes the law.

Distinguish Between...
Here you need to be able to explain the difference between one term or concept and another.

Annual General Meetings (AGMs) take place once a year (and must be held within 15 months of the previous one). Only public companies are obliged to have an AGM.

Distinguish Between ...

Extraordinary General Meetings – this is any meeting which is not an AGM. The directors can call an EGM at any time. However, substantial groups of shareholders can call an EGM within 28 days of the issue of notice to do so.

Doctor Proctor's Legal Language
Doctor Proctor gives you a legal definition and explains what it means in everyday terms.

A **contract** is a legal agreement between two or more parties, who promise to give and receive something from each other and who intend the agreement to be legally binding. In setting up a company it is important to create this contract between the organisation and its members so that everyone knows what they have contracted to, and any future disputes can be settled.

Doctor Proctor Outlines ...
Explanations of important themes and ideas in Business Law.

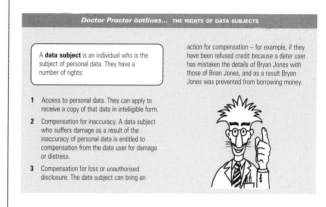

Doctor Proctor outlines... THE RIGHTS OF DATA SUBJECTS

A **data subject** is an individual who is the subject of personal data. They have a number of rights:

1 Access to personal data. They can apply to receive a copy of that data in intelligible form.

2 Compensation for inaccuracy. A data subject who suffers damage as a result of the inaccuracy of personal data is entitled to compensation from the data user for damage or distress.

3 Compensation for loss or unauthorised disclosure. The data subject can bring an

action for compensation – for example, if they have been refused credit because a dater user has mistaken the details of Bryan Jones with those of Brian Jones, and as a result Bryan Jones was prevented from borrowing money.

Doctor Proctor's Court Cases
Important elements of case law.

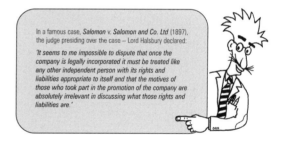

In a famous case, *Salomon v. Salomon and Co. Ltd* (1897), the judge presiding over the case – Lord Halsbury declared:

'It seems to me impossible to dispute that once the company is legally incorporated it must be treated like any other independent person with its rights and liabilities appropriate to itself and that the motives of those who took part in the promotion of the company are absolutely irrelevant in discussing what those rights and liabilities are.'

Questions and Answers
Short, practical exercises to test your understanding.

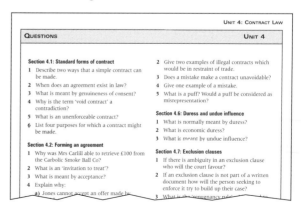

UNIT 4: CONTRACT LAW

QUESTIONS   **UNIT 4**

Section 4.1: Standard forms of contract
1 Describe two ways that a simple contract can be made.
2 When does an agreement exist in law?
3 What is meant by genuineness of consent?
4 Why is the term 'void contract' a contradiction?
5 What is an unenforceable contract?
6 List four purposes for which a contract might be made.

Section 4.2: Forming an agreement
1 Why was Mrs Carlill able to retrieve £100 from the Carbolic Smoke Ball Co?
2 What is an 'invitation to treat'?
3 What is meant by acceptance?
4 Explain why:
   a) Jones cannot accept an offer made by

2 Give two examples of illegal contracts which would be in restraint of trade.
3 Does a mistake make a contract unavoidable?
4 Give one example of a mistake.
5 What is a puff? Would a puff be considered as misrepresentation?

Section 4.6: Duress and undue influence
1 What is normally meant by duress?
2 What is economic duress?
3 What is meant by undue influence?

Section 4.7: Exclusion clauses
1 If there is ambiguity in an exclusion clause who will the court favour?
2 If an exclusion clause is not part of a written document how will the person seeking to enforce it try to build up their case?
3 What is the contingency rule...

UNIT 1

INTRODUCTION

This unit describes the way in which laws both constrain business activity and at the same time protect the business from a range of harmful practices. It then outlines the main sources of law that affect business including laws made in Parliament, case law decided in the courts, and the increasingly important impact of the European Union in creating a legal framework.

Topics covered in this unit

1.1 The main sources of law that affect business
Provides a brief description of the sources of law in this country and in the European Union.

1.2 Legislation by Act of Parliament
Describes and gives examples of the way in which Parliament can create new laws in this country.

1.3 Cases decided in the courts
The law courts exist to hear and pass judgement in areas involving disputes between organisations, and between individuals and organisations. These cases then establish a precedent governing a business and its relationships with the outside world.

1.4 European Union treaties, directives and regulations
As a member of the European Union, this country is bound to abide by treaties and legal guidelines established for all members of the Union. Businesses are increasingly having to keep an eye out for possible new changes in the law stemming from the EU in order to keep ahead of their rivals.

1.5 Civil and criminal law
Civil law governs disputes between individuals and organisations, whereas criminal law is concerned with dealing with cases where the laws of the country (i.e. criminal offences) appear to have been committed.

1.1 THE MAIN SOURCES OF LAW THAT AFFECT BUSINESS

Key Ideas

Law

There is no single commonly accepted definition of law, yet most people can recognise what law is involved with, for example, everyone can give you some examples of what it means to 'break the law'. Different definitions of law include 'rules of action' (Blackstone) and 'what officials do about disputes' (Llewelyn).

Generally speaking we can say that laws are widely accepted by most members of a society and provide a code of conduct for those people. For business people these laws provide controls as to what they can and cannot do in conducting their day-to-day lives and business activities.

In the course of time, laws may change so that business people need to keep up to date with legal requirements and with changes in the law both because it is right to do so and because there are often severe penalties for non-compliance.

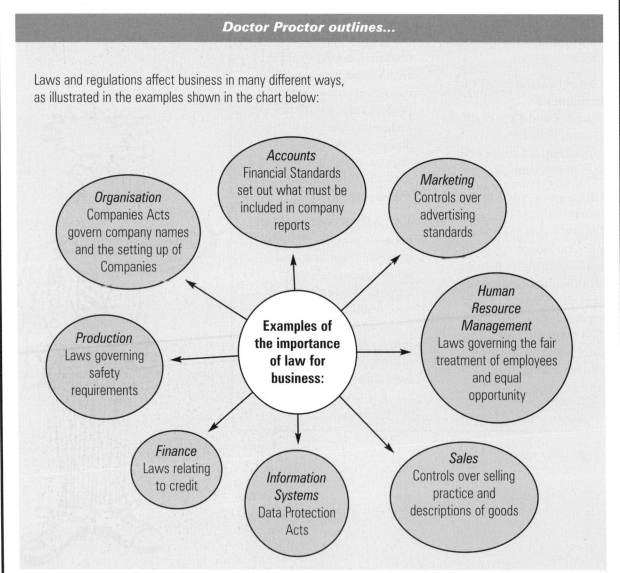

Doctor Proctor outlines...

Laws and regulations affect business in many different ways, as illustrated in the examples shown in the chart below:

Examples of the importance of law for business:

Accounts
Financial Standards set out what must be included in company reports

Marketing
Controls over advertising standards

Organisation
Companies Acts govern company names and the setting up of Companies

Human Resource Management
Laws governing the fair treatment of employees and equal opportunity

Production
Laws governing safety requirements

Finance
Laws relating to credit

Information Systems
Data Protection Acts

Sales
Controls over selling practice and descriptions of goods

1.1 THE MAIN SOURCES OF LAW THAT AFFECT BUSINESS

Dr Proctor says:
'You Must Know This!'

We use the term 'sources of law' to describe where laws come from, i.e. who makes the law.

2. **Laws made by judges** who build up principles over time on a case-by-case basis. This type of law is often referred to as 'common law'. Today, the European Union courts are also important in making judgments which have a widespread impact within the European Union. The principle of equity is important in underpinning judgments in common law.

Distinguish Between ...

There are two main sources of law:

1. **Legislation** – i.e. Acts of Parliament, and 'rules', 'regulations' and 'bye-laws' made by those who are given authority to legislate by parliament, e.g. local government bodies. Today, we are not just concerned with legislation in this country but also with European Union legislation.

Doctor Proctor outlines... THE PRINCIPLE OF EQUITY

The principle of equity is an important component of our legal system, which has been developed over time and is based on a sense of fair play. This is a belief in a form of natural justice – that the law needs to operate in a fair way. Equity is an important principle therefore assisting common law, and seeks to protect us all from 'crafty' misinterpretations of common law. Courts therefore seek solutions which are 'equitable'.

1.2 LEGISLATION BY ACT OF PARLIAMENT

Key Ideas 🔑

Act of Parliament

Many of the laws that affect business are framed by government, which has a responsibility for creating a suitable climate for business, for example, by passing new laws governing fairer competition, or limiting the way in which business can harm the environment.

An Act of Parliament is also sometimes called a Statute and is always set out in writing starting with the following introduction:

Be it enacted by the Queen's most Excellent Majesty, by and with the advice and consent of the Lords Spiritual and Temporal, and Commons, in this present Parliament assembled, and by the authority of the same as follows:

From reading the above statement you can see that a new law, perhaps one to protect consumers, involves the following:

1 Assent and signature by the Queen.
2 Advice and agreement from the House of Lords, and
3 Advice and agreement from the House of Commons.

Most new Acts of Parliament are put forward by the government of the day, although a small number are proposed by individual Members of Parliament – 'Private Member's Bills'.

There are a number of stages before a proposed change in the law becomes an Act of Parliament.

Stage

1 Bill proposed by government and put before Parliament for a formal first reading. No debate at this stage.

2 Bill given a second reading of the general principles of the bill. Debate and discussion takes place.

3 A committee of MPs will examine the bill, clause by clause, reviewing its details to see if they are acceptable and appropriate (committee of about 40-90 members). Amendments are proposed at this stage.

4 The report stage, where amendments made by committees are reported, and then taken on board or rejected.

5 Bill presented to House of Commons for a third time with any amendments from report stage. Brief debate.

6 Bill presented to House of Lords who can suggest amendments before returning it to the Commons. (As in the Commons there are three readings and a report stage.)

7 The Lords' amendments are considered by the Commons.

8 Bill is approved by the Queen (Royal Assent) and becomes law.

1.2 LEGISLATION BY ACT OF PARLIAMENT

The House of Commons is made up of 659 Members of Parliament who have been elected to represent a particular area known as a constituency. A majority of MPs must support the bill at each stage as it passes through Parliament. Generally speaking new laws will be approved but they may be amended on their way through the Commons and Lords. At any one time there will be a number of bills passing through Parliament, and business organisations need to follow what is happening in bills that affect them, so as to be ready to meet any new legal requirements.

Doctor Proctor explains... DELEGATED LEGISLATION

A number of laws that affect business are not created directly by central government but by bodies delegated to legislate by central government. Bye-laws are made by local authorities, which are bodies given the responsibility for regulating, administering and/or managing their districts, property or undertakings. Other bodies might also be allowed to create delegated legislation, e.g. public corporations – organisations set up by the government such as the BBC, or the Bank of England. The courts can make a judgment that a body has gone beyond the powers given to it by Parliament in creating delegated legislation – in which case the delegated legislation will be judged to be ultra vires ('beyond the powers') granted to that body.

1.3 CASES DECIDED IN THE COURTS

Key Ideas 🔑

Judicial precedent

Much of common law and equity is based on 'judgments' that have been made by judges. A judge hears a particular case, and passes a judgment. This then establishes 'case law', a precedent which other judges must follow. If this did not happen there would be chaos with nobody knowing where they stood with regards to the law. The concept of judicial precedent became firmly rooted as the basis for English law from the late nineteenth century onwards, although it had been in practice for a long time before.

In 1992 the signing of the Maastricht Treaty led to the creation of the European Union. This marked a significant milestone in European integration and involved handing over considerable powers for decision making to a supranational body, the European Union.

Doctor Proctor describes... THE HIERARCHY OF COURTS

The higher the court that makes a judgment, the more binding is the judicial precedent that is created. For example, the **Court of Justice of the European Union** is the highest court within the European Union, and courts may seek a ruling on points of European Union Law as a guide to conduct. The **Supreme Court** is the highest appeal court in this country, whose decisions are binding on lower level courts. In the course of time the Supreme Court may overturn previous decisions that it has made. The Supreme Court has been created as part of a process of modernising the judicial system.

At the next level is the **Court of Appeal** whose decisions are binding on all lower courts but which must bow to decisions made by the Supreme Court. The Court of Appeal typically consists of two or three judges.

The third level consists of the **High Court** whose decisions are made by judges, and whose decisions are more important than those of lower courts.

At the lowest level are the **county courts** whose job it is to deal with disputes between individuals and organisations. The work of these courts is administered by a Court Clerk and decisions are made by a judge, although sometimes a jury might be employed. **Magistrates' courts** have the responsibility for dealing with criminal cases where the law of the land has been broken. They are presided over by local magistrates who are appointed from respected members of the local community.

1.3 CASES DECIDED IN THE COURTS

Illustrating the hierarchy of Courts:

Note: In effect the House of Lords is typically the highest court of appeal in most cases, but where cases involve a European dimension, or cover areas covered by European Union legislation, then the European Union Court of Appeal will take precedent.

```
┌─────────────────────┐
│   European Union    │
│   Court of Justice  │
└─────────────────────┘
          │
          ▼
┌─────────────────────┐
│   House of Lords    │
│     Law Lords       │
└─────────────────────┘
          │
          ▼
┌─────────────────────┐
│   Court of Appeal   │
└─────────────────────┘
          │
          ▼
┌─────────────────────┐
│     High Court      │
└─────────────────────┘
      ↙         ↘
```

County Courts	Magistrates' Courts
(deal with disputes)	(deal with criminal cases)

The higher up is the court, the more important are the decisions it makes.

In addition, disputes can be taken to a small claims court. Here the case is dealt with by a process of arbitration. The advantage is that it doesn't involve the expense of other forms of court cases.

In making a decision a judge will explain the reasons (principles) behind his or her decision (**ratio decidendi**). It is these principles that create a precedent for other judges to follow.

This gives scope for decision making by future judges because they may feel that the principles set out do not fully cover the details of the case which they are subsequently dealing with. Therefore there is a need for a new **ratio decidendi** which builds on the previous one.

And, of course, a higher court might decide to overrule the **ratio decidendi** set out by a lower court judge. A higher court listening to an appeal can then, if it feels it is appropriate, overturn a decision made lower down.

1.3 CASES DECIDED IN THE COURTS

The advantages and disadvantages of Judicial Precedent:

Advantages

1. Provides a relatively clear body of precedents giving clear guidance for decision making.

2. Over time a detailed body of legal knowledge develops governing many differing disputes and situations.

3. The law is able to change over time and judges have the powers to build on previous decisions rather than having to resort to seeking guidance from 'higher authorities'.

Disadvantages

1. Previous decisions can stick in the legal system, restricting social change.

2. Because the law is hundreds of years old, often hundreds of previous rulings need to be examined, costing time and money.

The existence of judicial precedent in business law provides a wealth of guidance, and most business organisations will employ legal advisors at some stage to steer them through a range of important decisions governing such areas as setting up, or changing the organisation of a business, employee relations, product guarantees, health and safety requirements, consumer complaints, etc.

1.4 EUROPEAN UNION TREATIES, DIRECTIVES AND REGULATIONS

Key Ideas 🔑

European Union

The main objective of the European Union is that of creating European unification, based on the rule of law. The legal system of the European Union takes priority over national legislation. European Union law is made up of three types of legislation:

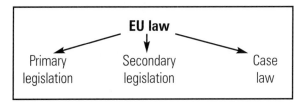

EU law
Primary legislation — Secondary legislation — Case law

Examples of such Treaties were the Single European Act (1987) creating a free trade area, and the Treaty of European Union (Maastricht Treaty 1993).

The Treaties set out the responsibilities of the various institutions of the European Union, e.g. the European Commission, the European Parliament, the Court of Appeal, and set out how laws will be made and applied within the Union.

Secondary legislation

This comprises the procedures set out in the various articles of the Treaty:

1. Regulations – these are directly binding on all Member States without the need for national legislation to put them in place.

2. Directives – these bind Member States to the objectives to be achieved within a certain time-limit, but leave national authorities to decide on how to implement them. Directives have to be implemented in national legislation.

3. Decisions – which are binding on relevant parties, e.g. government, businesses or individuals. They do not need to be implemented in national legislation.

4. Recommendations and opinions – these are not binding.

Primary legislation

This is made up of the Treaties and other agreements between member countries. This primary legislation was agreed upon by the parties concerned as a result of negotiations. These Treaties were then approved by the various Parliaments of the countries concerned.

Case law

Case law consists of judgments made by the European Court of Justice and of the European Court of First Instance, which result from referrals from the Commission of the European Union, national courts of the Member States or individuals.

1.4 EUROPEAN UNION TREATIES, DIRECTIVES AND REGULATIONS

For example, in January 2003, Spain and Italy were told by the European Court of Justice that they cannot label some of Britain's best known confectionery bars 'chocolate substitute', resolving a 30 year long dispute. The Court, which is based in Luxembourg, found the Spanish and Italian governments guilty of breaching EU trade laws by restricting the marketing of British chocolate. European Union legislation had established in 2000 that a small amount of vegetable fat is acceptable in chocolate products.

It tastes like chocolate to me!

Creating European Union law

The role of the Commission is to:

*   put forward new proposals for legislation,

*   safeguard the Treaties by making sure they are implemented and respected,

*   manage and carry out EU policies and oversee international trade relations.

Doctor Proctor outlines...

The drafting of new proposals for legislation is done by the European Commission which puts forward new suggestions for regulations or directives in line with various Treaties. The Treaties have given decision making powers to the European Union in a wide range of areas that are relevant to business including trade, the environment, consumer affairs, competition policy, research and development (R&D) policy, and economic and monetary union (EMU). European Commissioners are typically individuals who have played a significant role in the politics of their own country and in European politics.

As 'guardian of the Treaties' the Commission can initiate proceedings to make sure that Member States comply with their commitments and where necessary take the State, organisations or individuals to the Court of Justice. The Commission can fine individuals and groups who infringe Treaty Law.

An important role of the Commission which is relevant to business is that of enforcing the Treaty's competition rules and regulating mergers and acquisitions of companies above a certain size.

The Commission is answerable to the European Parliament which can dismiss it, or dismiss individual Commissioners.

Proposals for new legislation are put to the European Parliament and Council. The Council can amend certain proposals. The European Parliament shares the responsibility of co-decision with the Council in most areas.

The role of the European Council, which involves meetings of Government Ministers from Member States, is to examine proposals

1.4 EUROPEAN UNION TREATIES, DIRECTIVES AND REGULATIONS

put forward by the Commission. The Council can then adopt these proposals, amend them or ignore them.

Since the Maastricht Treaty the European Parliament has had powers of co-decision with the Council on many areas such as trading relations and consumer affairs.

The European Parliament is made up of Euro MPs who are directly elected within their own countries every five years. The European Parliament can amend and even adopt legislation.

The Amsterdam Treaty (1996) set out that decision making is shared between the European Parliament and the Council. Legislation is adopted in Council and the European Parliament agree at first reading. If there is disagreement a 'conciliation committee' made up of members of Council and European Parliament try to resolve the differences. If Parliament is not happy with the new proposals it can vote out the proposals.

Individual citizens and groups can put forward petitions to the European Parliament which represents their interests.

In practice most cases are heard in national courts. However, the European Court is there to safeguard the European Union's legal system.

The Court of First Instance was set up in 1989 to take some of the pressure off the European Court.

The European Court of Justice

Over the years the European Parliament has increasingly gained powers in terms of creating new legislation and this trend is likely to continue. Today the European Parliament can ask the Commission to put forward proposals for legislation.

Dr Proctor says:
'You Must Know This!'

The purpose of the European Court is to strengthen the protection of individuals under the law and to make sure that community laws are interpreted in the same way everywhere.

1.4 EUROPEAN UNION TREATIES, DIRECTIVES AND REGULATIONS

The Court takes decisions in situations involving disputes between:

- Member States
- The EU and Member States
- Institutions
- Individuals and the EU

It also provides opinions on international agreements.

The types of actions that the Court can take include:

- proceedings for failure to meet an obligation
- proceedings for failure to do something
- actions for damages
- appeals

In addition the Court makes preliminary rulings which help to make sure that the law is interpreted the same throughout the Union. These occur when a national court refers a dispute to the Court of Justice for a ruling. The Court also provides rulings in situations where Community law has been broken by a Member State.

The Court of First Instance makes judgments in the following areas:

- disputes involving the various European Union institutions
- actions brought against the Commission by undertakings or associations of undertakings
- actions brought against a European Union institution

1.5 CIVIL AND CRIMINAL LAW

Key Ideas 🔑

Civil disputes and criminal offences

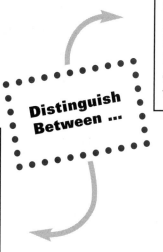
Distinguish Between ...

Criminal law is concerned with criminal offences where the law of the land has been broken. For example, if a lorry driver working for a local firm came into your house and stole a television set.

Civil law is concerned with disputes between individuals, organisations and other bodies. For example, you may have a dispute with a road haulage firm that drives heavy lorries past your house at all hours of the day and night.

Businesses need to be aware of the legal implications of both civil and criminal law. Frequently businesses do have disputes with individuals and other organisations. For example, they may not feel that the quality of raw materials supplied to them meets the standards they agreed with a supplier – a civil dispute. They may not be happy with the timekeeping of their employees – another civil dispute.

Where civil disputes can't be resolved by the parties concerned this may lead to a court case involving a civil court.

Type of civil court	Type of cases heard
Small claims court	Deals with 'relatively simple' cases involving disputes over such areas as non-payment of debts, unsatisfactory goods and services, etc. Dealt with by 'arbitration'. Normally initiated by the plaintiff rather than a solicitor.
County court	Involves more complex cases and larger sums of money than small claims court. Cases take longer to prepare. Dealt with by judge.
High Court	Deals with more complex cases than county court and ones involving large sums of money. Even longer preparation and deliberation. Dealt with by High Court Judge.

1.5 CIVIL AND CRIMINAL LAW

A number of criteria are taken into consideration in deciding what level of court should be involved including:

- Sums of money involved

- Complexity of the case

- Importance of case in establishing precedents

Minor criminal offences such as small scale pilfering from companies will typically be heard in a magistrates' court where trained magistrates picked from the local community are given advice by a court clerk. More serious cases are heard in the crown court which involves defence and prosecution solicitors. The crown court deals with all serious trials which are referred to as trials on indictment.

Criminal offences are classified according to degree of seriousness. The most serious cases such as murder will be tried by High Court Judges, while less serious cases are heard in the crown and magistrates' courts. It is possible to make appeals against sentence to a higher court.

Criminal cases

A survey in 2002 showed that record levels of fraud were taking place in companies, particularly by middle managers. Typical cases involved the fraudster obtaining the VAT (Value Added Tax) registration from another country to acquire VAT free goods, and then selling the goods on at VAT inclusive prices and pocketing the tax.

A civil case

In 2003 Swiss RE, a reinsurance company, took proceedings against Larry Silverstein, a property tycoon, for 'deliberately' underinsuring the World Trade Centre towers destroyed in the 11 September terrorist attacks. They claimed that he had not fully insured the towers in order to cut down his costs.

Section 1.1: The main sources of law that affect business

1 Who is responsible for making the two types of laws?

2 Why is the principle of equity important in underpinning our legal system?

Section 1.2: Legislation by Act of Parliament

1 Who is responsible for:

   a) Proposing a bill

   b) Examining the bill clause by clause

   c) Giving final assent for the bill?

2 Apart from the House of Commons, what other bodies have the powers to alter a bill before it becomes law?

3 Give one example of a body that is delegated the power from Parliament to make legislation.

4 What is meant by ultra vires?

Section 1.3: Cases decided in the courts

1 What is the highest court within the European Union?

2 What is the highest national court in this country?

3 What is the lowest level of criminal court?

4 Why is it important for judges to outline the principles involved in arriving at a decision?

5 Why might a business seek to take a court decision to a higher court for judgment?

Section 1.4: European Union treaties, directive and regulations

1 What is the difference between primary and secondary regulation?

2 Who can propose new legislation for the European Union?

3 Complete the following table by putting a tick in the first or second column and then filling in a comment in the third column:

	Directly binding	Not binding	Binding to whom?
Regulations			
Directives			
Decisions			
Recommendations			

4 What is the principal function of the European Court of Justice?

Section 1.5: Criminal and civil law

1 Which of the following instances would be tried in a criminal and which in a civil court?

   a) An employee is injured at work because her employer has ignored the requirements of the Health and Safety Act.

   b) A business claims that the quality of the raw materials that it has received is not as specified by the supplier.

   c) As a result of the takeover of one firm by another, the directors of one company claim that they should receive more compensation than they have been offered.

   d) An employee is found embezzling a firm's funds.

   e) A firm is in dispute with its employees about the length of time they are taking on tea breaks.

   f) A firm's drivers are found to be exceeding the number of hours that EU legislation specifies that they should drive in one session without taking a rest.

   g) One firm uses another firm's business name.

This unit gives a broad overview of the legal status of different types of business organisation in the private sector of the economy, i.e. organisations that are owned and run by private individuals rather than government concerns. It outlines the key features of different types of business organisation and the legal status of these concerns. The unit starts out with the smallest unit, the sole trader, before going on to examine partnerships, companies and charities.

Topics covered in this unit

2.1 Sole traders

Sole traders are owned by a single individual. They are thus relatively simple organisations, and are easier to set up than more complicated structures. The legal paperwork governing sole traders is also relatively simple.

2.2 Partnerships

The setting up and running of partnerships is governed by more detailed legislation than for the sole trader, as disputes may arise between the partners, and because relationships with third parties are likely to be more complex than in the case of the sole trader business.

2.3 Franchises

A franchise is a legal arrangement whereby one business (the franchisor) gives another (the franchisee) the right to use its trade name, and sell its products or services in a given geographical area. Legal frameworks covering franchising are important because disputes can arise between the parties concerned with the arrangement, and also with third parties.

2.4 Private and public companies

A company is owned by a group of shareholders who are given various legal protections. There is a key distinction between a private company whose shares can only be sold with the permission of the Board of Directors of the company, and public companies whose shares are sold freely on the Stock Exchange with less control over who buys them.

2.5 Charities

Charities are set up to do 'good works' and most operate within certain legal guidelines to keep their charitable status.

More details about the legal relations of each of the five organisations covered in this unit are set out in Unit 3 – Laws governing the formation and running of businesses.

2.1 SOLE TRADERS

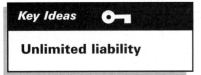

Key Ideas

Unlimited liability

A sole trader is the most common form of business ownership and the easiest to set up. A sole trader is a business owned by one person – though this business may employ a large number of people.

To start trading as a sole trader all you need to do is open your door, there is no complex paperwork to be filled in beforehand. In addition you can keep the affairs of your business private, because you are not required to publish reports – simply to fill in your tax return for the Inland Revenue each year.

Hi – my name is Sarah Rayfield. I work from home as a sole trader producing websites for big companies. The great thing is that I work for myself, make all my own decisions, and take all the profits of the business for myself.

Sole traders hope to make a profit. However, if a sole trader runs into debt, they will have to pay the money they owe from their own pocket. The business term we use to describe this position is **unlimited liability**.

When a sole trader business is set up, capital will be required to start and then run the business. Sole traders have their own resources to draw on, but that is all because they are on their own. If they want additional capital they will have to borrow it – perhaps from a bank.

For example, if a sole trader has business and equipment worth £25,000 and they run up debts of £50,000, the debt is not limited to the £25,000 which they have already put into the business. This means that if they are taken to a civil court they may have to sell their house and any other possessions they have to meet the debts.

2.1 SOLE TRADERS

Doctor Proctor outlines...

The legal advantages and disadvantages of being a sole trader are that:

Advantages

Easy to set up as no initial paper work required.

No reports required so business affairs can be kept private

Disadvantages

Unlimited liability

Like other businesses tax returns needed for Inland Revenue

Typical examples of sole traders are tradesmen such as plumbers and small building firms, graphic designers, providers of personal services such as mobile hairdressers, small shops, and a number of Information Technology services such as web page design.

Other advantages of being a sole trader are that:

- because the businesses are small, only a little capital is required,

- decision making can be done by a single individual,

- decisions can be made quickly,

- the individual owner is closely in touch with customers' needs and requirements.

2.2 PARTNERSHIPS

Key Ideas

Deed of partnership

A partnership is a business association between two or more owners of an enterprise. Partnerships usually have between two and twenty members, though there are some exceptions.

Partnerships are common in many types of business. They are usually found in small shop ownership and in professional practices such as vets, doctors, solicitors and dentists.

The usual way to start a partnership is to ask a solicitor to draw up a Deed of Partnership. This lays down how profits and losses are to be shared, and sets out the duties of each partner – for example, how much capital they should contribute, their roles and responsibilities, how profits will be taken out of the business, and procedures for introducing new partners and settling disputes.

The Partnership Act 1890

This Act sets out rules which partners can refer to if they are not already covered in the Deed of Partnership (or if a Deed has not been drawn up).

Limited or 'sleeping' partners can be introduced to a partnership. They have limited liability as long as they take no active part in the running of the business.

The Partnership Act of 2002 set out that in some cases it is possible to have limited liability partnerships (e.g. in accountancy firms).

Limited liability means that if a partnership runs into debt the maximum amount in law that partners are expected to lose is what they put into the business. However, with unlimited partnerships, partners can lose almost everything they own.

Hi, my name is Doctor Sanjay Patel. I am a GP and share a partnership practice with two other doctors. The advantage is that we can share out the workload, and each of us have different specialisms so that we can deal with most cases between us.

2.3 FRANCHISES

Doctor Proctor outlines...

A well known example of franchising is Coca-Cola, which franchises out its bottling arrangement. The following chart shows the responsibility of Coca-Cola and its franchisees:

Responsibility of Coca-Cola

Owner of the trade mark.

Supplier of syrups and key drinks ingredients.

Responsibility for global marketing and advertising to consumers.

Responsibility of franchisees

Management of sales.

Management of manufacturing.

Management of distribution.

The franchise agreement between the franchisor and the franchisee is very important because it determines the legal responsibility of each party and covers such areas as:

- how much will be contributed by each partner in setting up the business,

- division of profits, i.e. percentage to be paid to franchisor,

- responsibilities of both parties, e.g. training and equipment to be supplied by franchisor, percentage or amount of equipment/ materials that need to be bought by the franchisee from the franchisor, etc.,

- responsibilities of parties in dealing with third parties, e.g. responsibility to consumers and to employees.

It is easy to see that the franchising agreement needs to be very specific, because as there are two parties involved in franchising it would be easy for one party to claim that a particular aspect of trading is the other's responsibility.

2.4 PRIVATE AND PUBLIC COMPANIES

Key Ideas 🔑

Joint Stock Company

A company is a group of people who share responsibility for a business venture. The owners (shareholders) jointly put a stock of capital (money) into the business. They are then entitled to a share of the profits in the form of a dividend.

Doctor Proctor explains... HOW A COMPANY IS A LEGAL ENTITY IN ITS OWN RIGHT

An Act of Parliament of 1844 recognised all joint stock companies that registered under it as bodies in their own right. The **joint stock company** thus became a body which was separate in law from the individuals who owned the company.

Shareholders appoint a **Board of Directors** which has a collective responsibility for the stewardship of the company. The shareholders appoint directors to run the company on their behalf.

Executive directors are ones with a responsibility for putting decisions into practice. **Non-executive directors** are ones who provide advice to the Board and help the company through their contacts.

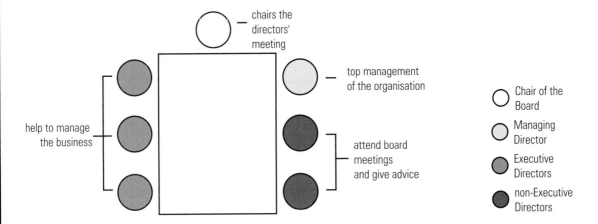

chairs the directors' meeting

top management of the organisation

help to manage the business

attend board meetings and give advice

○ Chair of the Board

◔ Managing Director

◒ Executive Directors

● non-Executive Directors

The Board of Directors has a collective responsibility for the stewardship of the company.

Shareholders play a role in appointing and dismissing directors. However, the managing director plays a key part in appointing executive directors, i.e. ones who are responsible for carrying out decisions within the company.

The chair and non-executive directors can play an important part in removing the managing director by voting on the Board. However, in law, directors can only be removed by shareholders.

2.4 PRIVATE AND PUBLIC COMPANIES

Directors are required to report each year about their stewardship of the company. Shareholders can attend the **Annual General Meeting** (AGM) and ask questions about the running of the business. Shareholders can vote at the AGM. Their voting rights are often proportionate to the number of shares they hold.

Shareholders vote to accept the annual report presented by the directors, and they can vote on the re-appointment of members of the Board.

Directors can appoint managers to manage the company on their behalf. Most companies are required to have at least two directors.

The **Chair of the Board** chairs directors' meetings and the AGM. However, the chair is often different from the managing director, who plays a key role in the management of the organisation.

> **Private companies** (Ltd companies). Shares in the company are sold privately with the permission of the Board of Directors. Typically private companies are small and medium-sized companies. However, there are some very big private companies like Mars the chocolate bar producer. Shareholders have the protection of limited liability.

Distinguish Between ...

> **Public companies**. These are companies whose shares are traded on the Stock Exchange. They are usually large companies and all shareholders have limited liability. Well known examples of PLCs are Marks and Spencer, Sainsbury's, Manchester United, and HMV.
>
> **Sainsbury's**
> making life taste better™
>
> **MARKS & SPENCER**

Doctor Proctor outlines... LIMITED LIABILITY

Shareholders in a company are given a very important legal protection known as limited liability. Limited liability means that should a company run into financial difficulties and run up debts, the maximum amount that the shareholders are liable to pay of this debt is the value of their shareholding. This means that although the shareholders are part owners of the company they will not be expected to sell off their personal possessions and property to pay the debts of the company.

2.5 CHARITIES

Charities provide a good example of a not-for-profit organisation whose purpose is different from the private sector businesses already examined. In recent times new government legislation has been introduced to tighten up what constitutes a charity. The prime aim of a charity should be to serve the wider community. As a result there has been criticism of a number of organisations that were using charitable status to avoid paying certain taxes. This loophole has been tightened.

Under new legislation the objects of a charity which are recognised as being lawful have been extended from four to ten. These are:

1 The prevention and relief of poverty.

2 The advancement of education.

3 The advancement of religion.

4 The advancement of health.

5 Social and community advancement.

6 The advancement of culture, arts and heritage.

7 The advancement of amateur sport.

8 The promotion of human rights, conflict resolution and reconciliation.

9 The advancement of environmental protection and improvement.

10 Other purposes beneficial to the community.

Typically the Trustees of a charity might consist of a President, Vice-President, Treasurer and Secretary and perhaps other officials.

Previously the supervision of charities was by the Charities Commission but it appears that this will be replaced by a Charity Regulation Authority which seeks to make sure that these organisations abide by the rules. These rules include, for example, that charities in this country must have a bank account here, and they need to show that they are benefiting the public. For example, it is suggested that some schools may lose their charitable status unless they can show that they are providing a benefit to the wider community rather than just to fee-paying students.

Doctor Proctor outlines... THE FEATURES OF A CHARITY

The key features of a charity are that:

- It is an organisation established for charitable purposes only.

- Its income must be applied to charitable purposes only.

- The people involved in decision making in a charity should be its trustee, directors or members of the management committee.

- Members of the charity should not receive dividends.

- If a charity dissolves then its assets should be distributed to another charity

2.5 CHARITIES

Dr Proctor says:
'You Must Know This!'

A 'public benefit test' for charitable status is one where the charity must show that its work is intended to benefit the general public or a reasonably large sector of the general public.

All charities whose income is above £10,000 per year must register. Those that fall below this benchmark are classified as 'Small Charities'. Charities must gain a local licence for local collection of money.

The new body responsible for supervising charities is creating a website with details of all the major charities. Examples of well known charities are:

As a result the following types of organisations would be excluded from charitable status:

- clubs run exclusively for a narrow group of members;

- organisations restricted to a narrow elite;

- building renovations carried out by organisations would also not qualify for charitable status if the buildings concerned excluded large groups of people.

Charities whose annual income is greater than £1 million must each year produce a standard information return including information about fundraising and the content of their work. They must also declare their ethical investment stance in this annual report.

Oxfam – an international charity that works with others to overcome poverty and suffering.

War Child – an international charity dedicated to improving the lives of children caught up in areas of conflict and war around the world.

Doctor Proctor outlines... THE BENEFITS OF CHARITABLE STATUS

There are important benefits to being registered as a charity. These include:

1 Credibility as a charity in fundraising.

2 Exemption from income tax, corporation tax and capital gains tax.

Section 2.1: Sole traders

a) What legal aspects of owning a sole trader business can be seen as disadvantages to adopting this form of business organisation?

b) Why might an individual choose this form of business organisation despite the legal disadvantages?

Section 2.2: Partnerships

1 Which of the following would you typically find in an ordinary partnership?

   a) A sleeping partner.

   b) Limited liability.

   c) At least two partners.

   d) Corporate status.

   e) Capital.

   f) Shareholders.

   g) Deed of Partnership.

   h) A set of accounts.

2 What legal documentation is usually involved in setting up a partnership? Who helps the partners to create this documentation?

3 What is the legal position of a Deed of Partnership should one of the partners die?

Section 2.3: Franchises

1 Who are the two partners in a franchise arrangement?

2 What would be the principal benefits to someone receiving a substantial redundancy payment from their previous job in taking out a franchise?

3 Why do you think that companies like Coca-Cola franchise out some of their operations such as bottling?

Section 2.4: Private and public companies

1 Who are the owners of a company?

2 Who do the owners of a company appoint to represent their interests?

3 What is the difference between the executive and the non-executive directors of a company?

4 Who plays the key role in appointing the directors of a public company?

5 How is the existence of limited liability likely to encourage more people to buy shares in companies?

6 What factors might lead shareholders to want to replace an existing Board of Directors in a company?

7 Which of the following is not a feature of a company?

   a) Limited liability.

   b) Partners.

   c) Directors.

   d) An Annual General Meeting.

   e) A Company Secretary.

   f) One owner.

Section 2.5: Charities

1 Give three examples of well known charities.

2 How does the legal status of a charity differ from that of a profit making enterprise?

3 Which of the following are features of charities?

   a) The ability to make profits.

   b) Concern for good causes.

   c) A Board of Trustees.

   d) No need to produce accounts.

   e) No organisation or management systems.

   f) They do not have Ltd or PLC after their name.

   g) They must register.

Topics covered in this unit

3.1 Memorandum and Articles of Association

All companies must register with the Registrar of Companies. The most important document setting out the internal working of the company is the articles of association, and the document setting out the company relations with the outside world is the memorandum of association.

3.2 Statutory books

The Companies Act requires companies to keep certain 'books'. In reality these are records rather than books as they don't have to be bound. These include a register of members, a register of directors, a register of the interests of directors, a register of company secretaries, copies of the memorandum and articles, and a register of charges.

3.3 Statutory contracts

The memorandum and articles, when registered, bind the company and its members to the same extent as if they had been signed and sealed by each member. The Companies Act does however allow for the changing of this contract in the course of time.

3.4 Partnership agreements

This section examines what is meant by a partnership and what it is that partners agree to do.

3.5 The Companies Acts 1985 and 1989

The Companies Acts bring together a host of legislation covering the way in which companies are allowed to be formed and run. These laws seek to provide clarification governing a range of situations and disputes that might potentially arise between a company, its members, and the outside world.

3.6 The Partnership Act 1890

The Partnership Act sets out the basic rules relating to this type of business organisation.

The law sets out a range of requirements and details of how businesses must be set up, including such aspects as the paperwork that needs to be registered, and what is acceptable as a lawful business name. This unit therefore starts out by outlining the legal requirements involved in setting up different types of business structure, and then goes on to examine relevant legislation such as the Companies Acts.

Topics covered in this unit

3.7 The Business Names Act 1985

Businesses can't simply choose to trade and operate under any name. There are tight rules about what is acceptable in law, both to protect the wider public against being misled and to protect other businesses with similar names.

3.8 Legal responsibilities of key personnel in a business

This section outlines the legal responsibilities of key personnel including the directors and company secretary of a company.

3.1 MEMORANDUM AND ARTICLES OF ASSOCIATION

Key Ideas 🔑

Registering as a company

The registration of company details is required to try to stop people selling false promises and making fraudulent claims about their business.

There are a number of important steps involved in forming a company. This is because it is important to protect individuals against unscrupulous practice.

This all stems back to the 'South Sea Bubble' and other scams in the nineteenth century. A number of individuals involved with the South Sea Company claimed to have found untold riches in the 'South Seas'. People rushed to buy shares in the company – which soon collapsed because it was a huge confidence trick.

This led to the creation of new laws including one related to limited liability to protect shareholders and others who have dealings with companies.

The upshot is that today all companies must be registered with the Registrar of Companies and must fill in key papers before being given a Certificate of Trading.

Promoters

Individuals wishing to set up a company are referred to as 'promoters'. There are two ways promoters can get a company formed.

1. They can employ a solicitor to 'tailor make' a new company for them. This involves filling in certain documents.

2. The solicitor can arrange the purchase of an 'off the peg' company for the promoters. This is a company that has already been 'incorporated' (all of the above has already been done) – and simply needs transferring to new owners. There are businesses that specialise in creating companies on paper and then selling these paper companies to new owners – i.e. the promoters of a new company.

```
        Promoters employ
        solicitor to create:
               │
               ▼
        Memorandum

        Articles

Details of registered office, directors, secretary

Declaration of compliance with Companies Act

        Payment of a fee
               │
               ▼
        Registered with
        registrar
```

3.1 MEMORANDUM AND ARTICLES OF ASSOCIATION

Memorandum of Association

The memorandum of association outlines the relationship of the company with the outside world. The Companies Act sets out that it must contain five compulsory clauses:

i)   The **name** of the company,
     e.g. Internet books.Com

ii) The **registered office**,
     e.g. England

iii) The **objects** of the company
     e.g. to market and sell books and
     periodicals over the Internet.

iv) The **liability** of the members,
     e.g. limited liability.

v)   The **authorised share capital** of the
     business,
     e.g. the company has been authorised to
     raise up to £250,000 in share capital.

The name of the company needs to have Ltd or PLC to show that the company has limited liability. In addition the company cannot use the name of an existing registered company, and it can't have anything offensive in its title, e.g. FU.UK.

The Secretary of State (Government Minister) can order a company to change its name if it is in breach of rules of decency or if it is too like a name already registered.

In the course of time a company can pass a special resolution to change its name.

The registered office of the company states where that office is, e.g. in England, Wales or Scotland. The address of the company is given elsewhere.

The objects clause sets out the purpose of the company and the powers that it has. The objects clause is expressed very widely because if a company carries out actions which go beyond these objects they might be declared ultra vires

(beyond the powers). In reality most companies will therefore set out objects which cover more or less anything that they want to do. For example, a general trading company may set out its objects as to:

'carry on any trade or business whatsoever'.

In the course of time a company can change its objects by a special resolution at the Annual General Meeting.

The liability clause sets out whether the members have limited or unlimited liability. Although most companies have limited liability it is possible to set up a company with unlimited liability – there are over 2,000 in the UK. All of these are private companies (you can't have a PLC with unlimited liability).

The capital clause sets out how much authorised capital a business has and perhaps how these shares are divided up into different types, e.g. preference shares and ordinary shares. The company cannot raise more capital than the authorised amount.

However, in the course of time this amount can be altered by agreement by the shareholders.

Articles of Association

The articles state the internal rules governing the company's organisation, including rules about meeting and the voting rights of shareholders. Also included is a list of directors and information on other internal matters. Shareholders can vote to change the articles.

There are no compulsory clauses for the articles, but the Companies Act sets out a standard set of articles which are thought of as being suitable to an 'average' company – referred to as Table A. A company therefore can set out its own articles or

3.1 MEMORANDUM AND ARTICLES OF ASSOCIATION

use Table A as the base. Table A is updated as the Companies Act is modified over time. In the course of time the articles can be updated.

Form 10

In addition to the memorandum and articles a business must produce Form 10 for registration. This form must contain the following:

- The address of the company's first registered office. Later this can be moved provided it is in the country stated in the memorandum.

- The company must list at least two officers – a company secretary, and a director. Typically companies will have more directors.

- Details of other directorships held by directors.

Form 12

Form 12 is for a statutory declaration by the solicitor who is employed to form the company, stating that all of the registration requirements have been complied with.

The Fee

These documents are then sent with a fee, which increases over time.

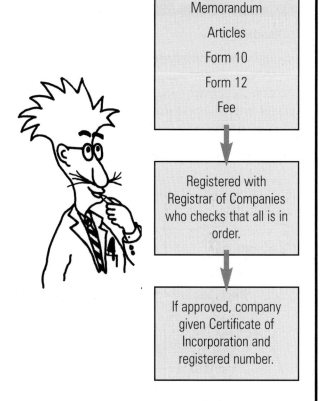

| Memorandum |
| Articles |
| Form 10 |
| Form 12 |
| Fee |

Registered with Registrar of Companies who checks that all is in order.

If approved, company given Certificate of Incorporation and registered number.

Key Ideas

Incorporation

A corporate body is one that is recognised in law in its own right – e.g. Marks and Spencer PLC, Tesco PLC, etc. A company or corporate body is established when the registrar provides a Certificate of Incorporation. A registered company will be given a registered number which needs to be quoted on all official documents and business letters.

When the registrar feels that all is correct, a Certificate of Incorporation will be granted enabling the company to became a legal body.

A registered company is then expected to display its registered name outside every office or place of business where it can be easily seen and read. The business name must then appear on all:

Business letters

Cheques

Invoices

Notices

Demands for payment

Failure to do the above can leave an officer of the company liable to a fine.

All order forms and letters made out by the company must contain the registered office of the company, the country in which it is registered, the registration number, and the fact that the company is limited.

3.2 STATUTORY BOOKS

Key Ideas 🔑

'Books'

The Companies Act requires companies to keep certain 'books'. These may be presented in actual form or just be filed paper records.

Statutory books are records that a company is obliged to keep by law so that the Registrar of Companies, company members and sometimes outsiders can be confident that the business is being conducted in a sound and businesslike way.

Inspecting the books

The organisation and affairs of companies are expected to be far more transparent than is the case, say, with a sole trader. Books therefore should be open to inspection by company members, creditors and the general public for at least two hours during the normal business day.

Other documents

Other documents which are available to public scrutiny include:

1   The minute book of general meetings, which can be examined only by company members.

2   A list of directors' service contracts, which again can only be examined by company members.

3   Copies of all documents which create a charge over the company's property. These documents are open to scrutiny by members and by creditors of a company free of charge. Other people can view these by paying a fee. It is easy to understand why creditors might want to look at liabilities that a company is building up because this might jeopardise the company's ability to meet its debts.

Doctor Proctor outlines... THE MAIN BOOKS THAT ARE REQUIRED ARE

---

1   A register of members. These are members of companies, i.e. shareholders, and the records which need to be kept about them are:

   • name
   • address
   • date of entry on register
   • date of termination of membership
   • shares held.

2   A register of directors, and register of secretaries. These records should set out the dates that these officials hold office, and:

   • name
   • address

   • details of other directorships (for directors only).

3   A register of the interests of directors. This sets out the shareholding and other interests of directors in the company, as well as subsidiary and holding companies. It must also include details of the interests of the family members of directors (because it would be possible for a director to hold shares in the name of a spouse or child).

4   Copies of the company's memorandum and articles.

3.3 STATUTORY CONTRACTS

Key Ideas 🔑

Contracts

A **contract** is a legal agreement between two or more parties, who promise to give and receive something from each other and who intend the agreement to be legally binding. In setting up a company it is important to create this contract between the organisation and its members so that everyone knows what they have contracted to, and any future disputes can be settled.

Before a company receives a Certificate of Incorporation, the solicitor representing the organisation must fill in a statutory declaration stating that all of the registration requirements have been complied with.

As a contract these documents provide rights and obligations between the organisation and the members:

1 The company can take legal action to enforce the contract upon its members.

2 Members can take legal action to enforce the contract on the company – for example, if the company is carrying out actions that go beyond what is set out in the articles.

3 Members of a company can also take legal action to enforce the contract on other members.

4 However, the articles of association of a company do not constitute a contract between a company and an outsider (i.e. a non-member). Nor do they give individual members special contractual rights beyond those of the members generally.

Doctor Proctor explains... WHAT IS MEANT BY A STATUTORY CONTRACT

Once the memorandum and articles have been registered, the company and its members are bound to the same extent as if they had been signed and sealed by each member and contained covenants on the part of each member to keep to the provisions of these documents.

The statutory contract relates to both the memorandum and the articles. Remember that if the company wants to change the contract then it can make alterations to the memorandum and articles provided that they are registered and communicated to the members. For example, the articles can be altered by a 'special resolution'.

3.4 PARTNERSHIP AGREEMENTS

Key Ideas 🔑

Partnership

The Partnership Act of 1890 defined a partnership as:

> *'the relationship which subsists between persons carrying on a business in common with a view of profit.'*

Persons who have entered into partnership are collectively called a firm, and the name under which they carry out business is referred to as the firm name, e.g. Patel, Smith, and Amin. In creating a partnership a contract is entered into between the partners, and this contract only becomes valid once the partnership has been formed.

A partnership agreement is usually set out with a solicitor, and is referred to as a Deed of Partnership. However, if the partners fail to register an agreement they are protected by the Partnership Act of 1890 which sets out details of partnership agreements.

Traditionally partnership agreements are most commonly found among groups of professional people, e.g. accountants, solicitors, and medical practitioners as well as some small business organisations such as retail outlets, plumbers, etc.

In recent years some partnerships have been growing in size; for example, there are huge accountancy firms, and groups of solicitors consisting of hundreds of partners. As a result new legislation was created in 2000 to provide a more suitable form of business organisation – the Limited Liability Partnership Act 2000.

To form a limited liability partnership:

- There must be at least two people who subscribe to the incorporation document. These details must be delivered to the registrar on a special form.

- The incorporation document must be delivered to the registrar.

Doctor Proctor outlines... THE LIMITED LIABILITY PARTNERSHIP ACT 2000

The Limited Liability Partnership Act starts out:

Be it enacted by the Queen's most Excellent Majesty, by and with the advice and consent of the Lords Spiritual and Temporal, and Commons, in this present Parliament assembled, and by the authority of the same, as follows:

1 There shall be a new form of legal entity to be known as a limited liability partnership.

2 A limited liability partnership is a body corporate (with legal personality separate from that of its members) which is formed by being incorporated under this Act.

3.4 PARTNERSHIP AGREEMENTS

The incorporation document must:

1	Be in a form approved by the registrar.

2	State the name of the limited liability partnership.

3	State the country in which the registered office of the partnership is to be found, e.g. Wales.

4	State the address of the registered office.

5	State the name and address of each of the partners.

6	State who are the designated members of the partnership.

Once the registrar is happy, a certificate of incorporation will be provided in the name specified in the incorporation document.

Once the partnership is established new members can become members of the partnership in agreement with existing partners. Existing members can leave the partnership.

Once the partnership is set up the members become agents of the partnership, and their actions are binding on the partnership if they are carried out in accordance with the partnership agreement.

A limited liability partnership therefore shares many common characteristics with other formers of incorporated business, but the members are the partners rather than shareholders.

3.5 THE COMPANIES ACTS 1985 AND 1989

Key Ideas

Limited by shares

The law relating to companies is mainly set out in the Companies Acts of 1985 and 1989 and in resulting case law.

In law a company is a 'corporation', i.e. it is recognised as a legal body in its own right. As a corporation a company can own property, can sue its debtors, is liable for its own debts and can be sued by creditors. It also has 'permanent succession', meaning that it does not have to be reformed when old members leave and new members join.

In other words we must see a company as a body in its own right, and treat it as such in law, rather than thinking of it as being made up of lots of separate individuals.

Types of Company
Limited by shares

Public and private limited companies are **'limited by shares'**. What this means is that the members/shareholders are liable to the debts of the company should it be liquidated – but only up to the value of their shareholding in the company.

In a famous case, *Salomon* v. *Salomon and Co. Ltd* (1897), the judge presiding over the case – Lord Halsbury – declared:

'It seems to me impossible to dispute that once the company is legally incorporated it must be treated like any other independent person with its rights and liabilities appropriate to itself and that the motives of those who took part in the promotion of the company are absolutely irrelevant in discussing what those rights and liabilities are.'

Differences between a public and a private company:

Public	Private
Can only start in business with a given minimum amount of share capital.	Does not have to have minimum amount of authorised share capital.
Can issue shares and debentures to wider public.	Cannot issue shares and debentures to wider public.
Has PLC after name.	Has Ltd after name.
Must have at least two directors.	Only needs one director.

3.5 THE COMPANIES ACTS 1985 AND 1989

Limited by guarantee

In addition there are some companies which are **'limited by guarantee'**. In these companies liability is restricted to what is set out in a clause of the memorandum. This clause states how much members of the company should be liable to should the company be wound up. Companies limited by guarantee do not raise money through share capital, but by members' subscriptions as might be the case in a sports club.

Unlimited companies

In addition there are a small number of **unlimited companies**, i.e. there is no limit to the liability of members. For example, companies trading on the Stock Exchange (as opposed to companies whose shares are traded on the Stock Exchange) have unlimited liability because the governing body of the Stock Exchange requires these companies to meet their own debts.

One of the main reasons that people hold shares is to take a share in the profits of the company in the form of a dividend.

There are four main things that a company can do with its profits:

1 Retain them in the business – 'ploughed back' profit.

2 Distribute them to shareholders as dividends.

3 Use them to pay directors' fees.

4 Use them to pay interest on loans known as debentures.

The company does not have a free choice as to how to distribute its profits. For example, it is contractually bound to pay interest to debenture holders (outsiders who have lent the company money), and to pay directors' fees. In addition it makes sound commercial sense to plough back some profits to improve the business for the future.

Doctor Proctor outlines... MEMBERSHIP OF A COMPANY

Individuals can become members of a company by buying new shares, buying existing shares off another member, or inheriting shares when a member dies.

Every company must keep a register of shareholders, including such details as:

- The date at which a member entered the register.

- Their name and address.

- The number of shares they hold.

- The dates at which individuals cease to be members.

The powers of the shareholders depend on how many shares they have. The company is run by its directors rather than the shareholders, but a majority shareholder, or a majority of shareholders, can vote to replace the board.

3.5 THE COMPANIES ACTS 1985 AND 1989

Doctor Proctor explains... HOW COMPANIES PAY DIVIDENDS

The shareholders are the owners of the company. Most companies seek to create 'shareholder value', i.e. good dividend returns on shares. The directors are responsible for declaring a dividend for shareholders. This may be an interim dividend (e.g. at six months) and an annual dividend. The directors will pay an interim dividend if it appears to be 'justified by the profits of the company available for distribution'.

The end of year dividend will be decided after the directors have examined the annual accounts for the business and will be recommended at the Annual General Meeting.

At the AGM the shareholders can accept the directors' recommendation, or they can vote for a dividend smaller than that recommended. By law they are prevented from voting for a dividend higher than that recommended.

The amount of dividend that a shareholder receives depends on the nominal value of the share, i.e. the face value of the share when it was issued. For example if a share has a nominal value of £1.00 and the dividend is 5%, the shareholder will receive 5p for each share held.

Doctor Proctor outlines... THE RIGHTS OF SHAREHOLDERS

Shareholders are entitled in law to:

- Transfer shares – i.e. to sell them on subject to any restrictions set out in the articles.

- Receive notice of meetings, attend meetings and vote (they can appoint a proxy to attend a meeting and vote on their behalf).

- Receive dividends, subject to the company being able to pay a dividend.

- Receive a copy of the annual report of the company within seven months of the end of the company financial year

3.5 THE COMPANIES ACTS 1985 AND 1989

Protecting shareholders

Case law governs the relationship between the minority and the majority of shareholders in a company. We can illustrate this first by the case of *Foss* v. *Harbottle* (1843).

A civil case involves a dispute between the plaintiffs – people making a complaint, and defendants – those making a defence of their actions.

In this case the plaintiffs were named Foss and Turton and they were shareholders in 'The Victoria Park Company' which was set up to buy land for use as a pleasure park. The defendants in this case were the directors and other shareholders in the company. Foss and Turton alleged that the defendants (Harbottle and others) had defrauded the company, for example, by selling off land belonging to the company to make money without letting the members of the company know. Foss and Turton sued on behalf of the company. However, the court decided that since it was possible that a simple majority of shareholders at a general meeting might have allowed the defendants to keep the alleged profits, the court would allow the defendants to keep the alleged profits. The company therefore was given priority over the minority of company members.

However, this rule of the majority does not apply where the company has personally wronged shareholders. This is illustrated by another case, *Pender* v. *Lushington* (1877). In this case the plaintiff, Pender, complained that the chair of the company was not allowing him to exercise his voting rights. In this case the courts backed the plaintiff.

There are a number of exceptions to the Foss case based on the majority getting their way on behalf of the company. These include:

1   Situations where the actions of the majority are ultra vires, e.g. directors going beyond the powers given to them in the articles.

2   The directors or others engaging in fraud to the detriment of the minority.

3.5 THE COMPANIES ACTS 1985 AND 1989

Company finance

There are two main types of share: ordinary and preference. Each offers different rights to dividends (returns) and capital repayment.

Ordinary shares

Holders of ordinary shares are entitled to a share in the profits of the business after all other investors have been paid their dues. They are able to vote at general meetings of the company and to exert influence in direct proportion to the number of shares they hold.

Items requiring shareholder authorisation include:

- the appointment of the board of directors

- the amount of profits distributed by way of dividend to the shareholders

- the issue or repurchase of share capital.

Ordinary share capital is often called 'equity capital' and can be likened to owner's equity in a private house. Equity for the householder is the difference between the value of the house and the mortgage secured against it. In the case of a company, equity (the value of ordinary shares) represents the difference between the value of assets owned by the business and the value of any outstanding loans and liabilities to other parties.

Example

	£000s
Assets	2,000
Liabilities	500
Equity	1,500

Preference shares

Holders of preference shares are entitled to receive a fixed dividend out of profits before payment is made to ordinary shareholders. But they usually have no voting rights, and so have less influence on company policy.

A company can buy back shares providing shareholders agree to sell them back. Sometimes a company issues redeemable shares where the capital sum is due to be paid back after a certain date.

The directors of a company cannot issue shares without the permission of the shareholders.

Authorised capital: the maximum number of shares the directors can issue according to the company's memorandum of association (a legal document drawn up when a company is established).

Distinguish Between ...

Issued capital: the number and nominal value of the shares actually issued to shareholders.

3.5 THE COMPANIES ACTS 1985 AND 1989

Borrowing

There is a danger that a company may borrow too much money, build up unmanageable debts and then be forced into liquidation.

The Companies Acts also govern the borrowing activities of companies. A company is allowed to borrow money for the purposes of its trade. It will also typically have the power to give security for the loan. However, the articles of a company may restrict the ability of directors to make 'substantial' loans on the company's behalf.

Companies can issue a debenture as a form of loan. A debenture is simply a document which acknowledges indebtedness by a company arising from a loan.

The term fixed charge refers to a mortgage of a particular asset. The company is not free to dispose of the asset without the consent of the mortgagee. A floating charge is a charge on other assets of a company which can be sold, e.g. stocks of goods, which are continually being sold and replaced.

When a bank, or other lender, lends money to a company it will usually require a fixed charge over any land or other property owned by the company. A register of all charges created by a company must be kept at Companies House, setting out:

- the date of the creation of the charge

- the amount secured by the charge

- brief particulars of the property charged

- the person entitled to the charge.

In addition the company must keep a register of all the charges affecting its property at its registered office. Failure to keep this record can result in a fine.

Company meetings

The Companies Acts also set out requirements relating to company meetings.

Annual General Meetings (AGMs) take place once a year (and must be held within 15 months of the previous one). Only public companies are obliged to have an AGM.

Distinguish Between ...

Extraordinary General Meetings – this is any meeting which is not an AGM. The directors can call an EGM at any time. However, substantial groups of shareholders can call an EGM within 28 days of the issue of notice to do so.

The transaction of business in a company meeting involves one of four types of resolution:

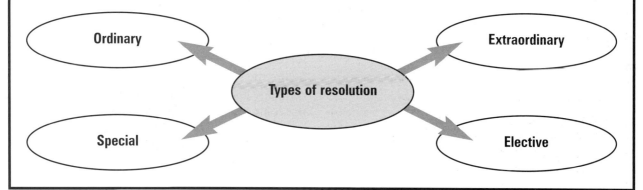

Ordinary   Extraordinary

Types of resolution

Special   Elective

3.5 THE COMPANIES ACTS 1985 AND 1989

An **ordinary resolution** is one that requires a majority of over 50% of shareholders. If the vote is tied 50-50 the articles of the company may give the Chair a casting vote to decide the issue.

Special and **extraordinary** resolutions require a 75% majority. A special resolution requires 21 days notice whereas an extraordinary resolution requires 14 days for an EGM and 21 for an AGM.

The Companies Acts set out when a special resolution is required, for example to change the articles or objects of the organisation.

An extraordinary resolution may be required to protect the interests of minority shareholders, for example, where a resolution is passed to commence a voluntary winding-up of the company because of its liabilities.

An **elective resolution** enables a private company to simplify its own internal management. It requires the unanimous approval of all the shareholders.

Company accounts

Dr Proctor says:

'You Must Know This!'

The Companies Acts also state that companies must keep 'accounting records'. The term accounting records refers to the keeping of sales invoices, purchase invoices, cheque books, paying-in books and bank statements as well as the financial accounts of the company. The obligation to keep these records rests with the company.

An independent auditor's report states whether proper accounting records have been kept.

A company's accounting records should be kept at its registered office or such other place as the directors think fit, and at all times should be open to inspection by the company's officers.

The accounts are expected to:

> **a)** disclose with reasonable accuracy the financial position of the business at intervals of not more than six months, and
>
> **b)** enable the directors to make sure that the company's balance sheet and profit and loss account comply with the Companies Acts.

Failure to keep records is an offence and can lead to company directors being disqualified from office.

As well as providing accounting records of individual companies, records must be kept of the accounts of a group of companies.

A company's annual accounts need to be approved by the board of directors and signed on behalf of the board by a director of the company. The signature appears on the company's balance sheet. The signed balance sheet must be delivered to the Registrar of Companies.

In addition a directors' report must be produced each year which must be signed by a director or secretary of the company. This report will be laid before the company at a general meeting. The company auditor's report will also be laid before the company in general meeting and state whether in their view the annual accounts have been properly prepared in accordance with the Companies Acts.

3.5 THE COMPANIES ACTS 1985 AND 1989

Dr Proctor says:
'You Must Know This!'

A copy of the company's annual accounts, together with a copy of the directors' report for that financial year and of the auditor's report of these accounts, must be sent to:

i) Every member of the company.

ii) Every holder of the company's debentures.

iii) Every person who is entitled to receive notice of general meetings.

These must be sent not less than 21 days before the meeting at which these documents will be presented to members.

Company insolvency

Insolvency occurs when a business is unable to meet its debts (liabilities).

Legislation regarding insolvency is designed to enable companies to keep functioning as going concerns, and to secure the preservation of jobs. If a company is forced to stop its activities it is much more difficult to start up again – hence the emphasis on keeping it going. There are a number of officials who take responsibility in cases involving insolvency.

An administrator

When a company gets into financial (or other) difficulties then the members, directors or creditors of a company may petition for an administrator to be appointed.

The Insolvency Act gives an administrator powers to manage the company, and then hopefully hand it over to a new permanent management team. The major responsibility of the administrator is to set out proposals for the administration of a company before a meeting of creditors. Copies of this plan also go to the Registrar of Companies and the shareholders.

A receiver

A receiver is a person who has a legal right to receive property belonging to another individual or body. For example, if you have debentures in a company, and the company fails to pay you the interest within a given period, then you could apply to the courts to appoint a receiver who will then take over some of the company's property or goods and sell it so that they can obtain for you your interest payments.

An **administrative receiver** combines the role of administrator and receiver and may be appointed when a bank is seeking loan repayments from a company. The administrative receiver will seek to manage the whole company while at the same time selling off items to secure repayment of debts.

A liquidator

This is a more drastic state of affairs where a liquidator will be appointed to sell off the company's assets to pay the debts of the company. Any balance will be returned to shareholders.

Companies can be wound up voluntarily by a special resolution of members, or by an extraordinary resolution whereby members recognise that the company will not be able to meet its liabilities.

You can see the problems of businesses getting into debt. In early 2003 Port Vale football club got into so much debt (£2.4m) that their creditors called in the administrator. The administrator was duty bound to get the money back for the creditors – including the prospect of the sale of Port Vale's ground.

3.6 THE PARTNERSHIP ACT 1890

Key Ideas

Powers of partners

In a partnership each partner is an agent of the firm and of his or her other partners. The business acts of these partners therefore bind the firm and the other partners (providing they are not ultra vires).

Doctor Proctor describes... THE LIABILITY SITUATION

Every partner is jointly liable for all the debts and obligations of the firm during the time that they are partners.

Where a partner is representing the partnership, then what he or she does or does not do which causes any form of injury is the shared responsibility of the partners.

Relationships between the partners

It is up to the partners to enter into a Deed of Partnership drawn up with a solicitor setting out arrangements. However, if this is not done the 1890 Partnership Act provides the framework for relationships between partners as set out below.

All of the property, and rights and interests in property which are brought into the partnership, or which are bought for the partnership by the firm, are referred to as the partnership property.

Property bought with money belonging to the firm is regarded in law as belonging to the firm.

The interests of partners in the partnership property and their rights and duties in relation to the partnership are illustrated below.

Doctor Proctor outlines... THE PARTNERS' RIGHTS AND DUTIES

1 All the partners are entitled to share equally in the capital and profits of the business, and must contribute equally to the losses.

2 Any partner who put in more money to the partnership (e.g. in making a payment) beyond the amount of capital he or she has agreed to subscribe is entitled to interest on this contribution.

3 Every partner may take part in the management of the partnership.

4 No new partner can join without the consent of all existing partners.

5 Disputes must be settled by a majority of partners.

6 The partnership books have to be kept at the place of business of the partnership.

7 A majority of partners can't expel other partners unless there is a legal arrangement to do so.

8 A partnership is dissolved on the death of a partner.

9 If a partnership dissolves, any losses must be first paid out of any profits, then out of the capital of the partnership, and finally out of the personal possessions/wealth of the partners in the proportion that they normally shared profits.

3.6 THE PARTNERSHIP ACT 1890

Types of partners
There are typically three main types of partners in a partnership.

1

General partners are the usual form of partner who have the right to take part in the management of the firm. In a partnership agreement there may be some restrictions of what partners can do, for example, junior partners may not be able to sign cheques.

2

Dormant or sleeping partners are individuals who put money into the business but are not involved in the day-to-day management of the business. For example, when a shopkeeper hands over their running of the shop to a son or daughter they may retain an interest as a dormant partner.

3

Salaried partners are individuals employed, for example, by accountants or solicitors for a salary rather than sharing in the profits of the business. They are really employees of the firm.

3.7 THE BUSINESS NAMES ACT 1985

Key Ideas

Appropriate names

There is no way that you would get away with calling your company *The Bloody Awful Dentists Government Bank*!

The law sets out clear requirements as to the naming of companies so that some names are allowed and others are prohibited.

The name of a public company must end with the words 'public limited company' or if it is registered in Wales its equivalent in Welsh ('cwmni cyfyngedig cyhoeddus'). A private company must typically have 'limited' 'cyfyngedig' after its name.

Companies are not allowed to use names (except with the approval of the Secretary of State) which give the impression that they are associated with the government or local government.

Companies are not allowed to use the 'same' name as one already registered. A company is likely to be asked to change its name if it is in breach of this requirement.

Companies may also not be allowed to use a name which is 'too similar' to an existing name. For example, if a company wanted to use the name 'The Body Shops' or 'Virgins Records' simply by adding an 's' to an existing name they would be likely to be stopped.

The use of certain names such as 'Bank' or 'Building Society' without authorisation may be a criminal offence, as may be the use of the titles of various professions such as 'Dentist', 'Optician', 'Pharmacist'.

Some names are also considered offensive and wouldn't be allowed – you can imagine what these might be!

If a company feels that another company is using the same name or a 'too similar' name they can take action through the civil courts.

Companies can change their name by special resolution.

Doctor Proctor outlines...
OPPORTUNISTIC USE OF NAMES

In recent years there have been quite a number of opportunistic registrations of company names. This occurs when a company takes on a name which they then hope to be able to sell on at a profit.

If in the Secretary of State's opinion the name by which a company is registered gives so misleading an indication of the nature of its activities as to be likely to cause harm to the public, he or she may direct it to change its name. Typically this direction must be complied with within six weeks (although a company can appeal).

If a company registers a name which includes a registered trade mark of another business, it is open to an action for infringement of the trade mark. As a result it is important for someone representing the company to inspect the trade mark register beforehand.

3.7 THE BUSINESS NAMES ACT 1985

For example, in the case of *Glaxo plc* v. *GlaxoWellcome Ltd* (1996), some opportunist business people anticipated the merger of Glaxo and Wellcome. The defendants in this case set up a company with the name Glaxowellcome knowing that the two companies were hoping to use this name.

The defendants were willing to sell the name GlaxoWellcome for £100,000.

However, in court the judge held that the defendants had acted dishonestly and that they had sought by unfair means to take for themselves the goodwill (and money) of the plaintiffs. In his judgement he set out that:

'The court will not countenance any such pre-emptive strike of registering companies with names where others have the goodwill in those names, and the registering party then demanding a price for changing the names. It is an abuse of the system of registration of companies' names. The right to choose the name with which a company is registered is not given for that purpose.'

Doctor Proctor outlines... THE LAW ON PARTNERSHIP NAMES

Partnership names

A partnership is allowed free use of certain names and approval for others under the Business Names Act. The partnership name in an ordinary partnership does not have to be registered with the Registrar.

Names which are freely allowed include names consisting of the surnames of all the partners. In addition it is permissible to use the partners' names with certain additions. Permitted additions include:

1   Forenames or initials of partners.

2   Addition of an 's' to a surname to show that there is more than one partner with the name, e.g. Patels rather than Patel.

3   A statement that the business is being carried on in succession of a former owner.

Where the business name is different in some form from the names of the partners then there are certain disclosure requirements that the name of each partner and an address for service must appear on:

- every business letter
- invoices
- orders for goods or services
- written demands for payment
- receipts.

This information must also be displayed in a prominent position at each place where the partnership is based.

For large partnerships a single address needs to be supplied rather than the address of each individual partner. As with companies it is unlawful to use a partnership name that implies a connection with government (except with approval from the Secretary of State).

3.8 LEGAL RESPONSIBILITIES OF KEY PERSONNEL IN A BUSINESS

Key Ideas

Directors

When a company sets up it will appoint a number of **first directors** and in the course of time some of these directors will retire or be removed and others will replace them. The minimum number of directors allowed by the Companies Act is two and there is no maximum number. An ordinary resolution can be used to change the number of directors.

Directors are appointed by a simple majority of members at company meeting or by unanimous written agreement.

Powers of directors

The powers of directors are set out in the articles of association and typically involve the power to manage the business of the company.

The decisions made by directors are typically made in a board meeting at which a quorum is present (a minimum number of directors set out in the articles), or by unanimous agreement. However, some decisions can be delegated to individual directors or managers

Decisions at board meetings are made by majority vote with the chair having a casting vote. Generally speaking directors are not allowed to vote on issues where they have a personal interest.

Statutory duties over directors

There is tight legal control relating to the disclosure of information about directors:

1   A register of directors must set out their names, addresses, and occupations, as well as directorships they hold in other companies.

Doctor Proctor outlines... THE RESPONSIBILITIES OF DIRECTORS

Directors owe what is known as a fiduciary responsibility to their organisation – in other words they act as trustees for their organisation. They must act responsibly for the benefit of the company and not make secret profit through their position.

Directors can receive payment for their work and often this payment is substantial. However, they must not profiteer at the expense of the company. The notion of secret profit suggests that a director carries out an activity as if he or she were working on behalf of the company, where really they are feathering their own nest (profiteering), without obtaining permission from the company to do so. Secret profits must by law be paid over to the company.

Other aspects of fiduciary responsibility are that:

1   The directors must only exercise their powers for the purpose for which they were given.

2   They must not exercise their powers for personal gain.

3.8 LEGAL RESPONSIBILITIES OF KEY PERSONNEL IN A BUSINESS

2 Directors must disclose their interest in a company, e.g. how many shares and debentures they hold. In addition, information must be disclosed about the interests of the spouse and children of directors so that members can see the influence a family holds.

3 Copies of the service contract of a director with a company must be readily available for members to scrutinise.

4 Directors must disclose their interest in particular contracts at Board meetings. This makes it apparent when a director stands to gain from a contract that a company makes with another organisation.

5 There are limitations on the loans that a company can make to directors.

6 If a director seeks to purchase some of the assets, e.g. property, of a company this requires approval at a shareholders meeting.

Directors can be removed from office by an ordinary resolution. Shareholders wishing to propose such a resolution must give 'special notice' of the resolution at least 28 days before a meeting at which the resolution will be discussed. However, it is often expensive to remove directors as they are entitled to compensation provided they have kept within the framework of the law.

The Company Secretary

The Companies Act requires that every company should have a Secretary. The Company Secretary is typically a director of the company. The role of the Secretary is to keep the records of the company which must be kept at the company office. It is a very responsible post and subject to fines if the company fails to comply with registration requirements. The Secretary is often responsible for key administrative work for the company – sending out notices about meetings, keeping the share register updated, etc.

Doctor Proctor outlines... THE POSITION OF MANAGING DIRECTOR

In many companies one of the directors will be appointed as Managing Director. This means that he or she will be the most senior director of the company or will be second in command to the Chair of the company. The powers of the Managing Director will be set out by the Board of Directors.

Typically the Managing Director will have a service contract to work for the company so that they are both an employee (manager) of the company and a director.

Section 3.1: Memorandum and Articles of Association

1   Who are the promoters of a company and what are the two ways that they can get companies formed?

2   List five items that would appear in the Memorandum. Who would be interested in the Memorandum?

3   What is meant by 'ultra vires'?

4   What are the articles and who are they for?

Section 3.2: Statutory books

1   What are the main types of statutory books?

2   Who is entitled to view the statutory books of a company?

Section 3.3: Statutory contracts

1   What is a contract?

2   What is a statutory contract?

3   Who do the articles of association provide a contract between?

Section 3.4: Partnership agreements

1   Define the term partnership.

2   What is a limited liability partnership?

3   Do limited liability partnerships have similarities with companies?

Section 3.5: The Companies Acts 1985 and 1989

1   What is meant by corporate status?

2   What was the significance of the *Salomon* v. *Salomon and Co. Ltd* case?

3   What is the difference between a company limited by shares and one limited by guarantee?

4   Who are the members of a company and what details need to be kept about them?

5   List four main rights of shareholders in relation to their Company.

6   What are the two main types of company meeting?

7   What is an ordinary resolution?

8   Give one example of a situation in which a special resolution may be brought into play.

9   Outline three legal requirements related to the production of company accounts.

10 What is the difference between an administrator and a receiver?

11 What is meant by maintaining a business as a 'going concern'?

Section 3.6: The Partnership Act 1890

1   Who is liable for the debts of a partnership?

2   Who owns the property brought into a partnership?

3   How are the profits of a partnership expected to be shared under conditions set out in the Partnership Act?

4   What conditions need to be agreed with for a new partner to join a partnership?

5   How are disputes settled between partners under the Partnership Act?

6   What sort of people are likely to be a) dormant partners, and b) salaried partners?

Section 3.7: The Business Names Act 1985

1   What basic requirements outline what is acceptable in the business name of a public limited company?

2   How can companies change their name?

3   Give examples of situations under which company names would be unacceptable.

4   What is the legal position with regards to the opportunistic use of business names?

5   What sorts of names are freely permissible for a partnership?

Section 3.8: Legal responsibilities of key personnel in a business

1   What is a first director?

2   How are new directors appointed?

3   What do you understand by the term 'fiduciary responsibility' of a director?

4   What is the main duty of a director?

5   List three types of information that must be disclosed about company directors.

6   Who appoints the Managing Director of a company?

7   What is the role of the Company Secretary?

Topics covered in this unit

4.1 Standard forms of contract
Explains what a contract is and the main forms of contract that are typically found in business relations – speciality contracts and simple contracts.

4.2 Forming an agreement
The first requirement for a contract is an agreement which involves at least two parties. The offeror makes an offer to the other party, known as the offeree. When the offeree accepts, an agreement is formed.

4.3 Capacity to contract and intention to create legal relations
Contracts can only be formed when individuals have the capacity to form contracts. This excludes minors (those under 18) and people who are mentally impaired in some situations. Directors can only form contracts on the behalf of their organisation if this is within their powers in the articles.

4.4 Consideration
Consideration is the process of making an exchange in a bargain where two or more parties provide each other with benefits.

4.5 Illegality
If a contract requires one or both parties to act in an illegal way then the courts will not uphold the contract.

4.6 Duress and undue influence
Duress involves situations of threatened or actual physical violence or where commercial pressure is being applied.

4.7 Exclusion clauses
The courts generally frown on exclusion clauses which set out to enable one party to a contract to avoid liabilities that they would otherwise carry.

4.8 Express and implied terms
The terms within a contract set out many of the statements made by parties to an agreement during negotiation of that agreement. These are

Contracts are formed every day when businesses carry out their activities and customers buy products or services. You need to appreciate the basic principles of contract law which are set out in this unit.

Topics covered in this unit

referred to as express terms. In addition, there may be a number of implied terms which are not strictly written into the contract but may relate to understanding about current legislation, e.g. relating to the sale of goods.

4.9 Termination of contract

This section outlines the four main ways that contracts are brought to an end (discharged).

4.10 Arbitration

Increasingly, where there are disputes between parties to a contract, these can be settled through an arbitration process in the civil courts rather than a full blown legal case.

4.11 Remedies

The law has established a number of remedies which are applicable to breach of contract and to the award of damages.

4.12 The Misrepresentation Act 1967

Misrepresentation is the false statement of a fact which induces another party to engage in a contract. The Misrepresentation Act sets out remedies for these situations.

4.13 The Unfair Contract Terms Act 1977

This Act relates to unfair terms which are set out in contracts and how they should be dealt with in law.

4.14 The Unfair Terms in Consumer Contracts Regulations 1999

This act relates to five main areas relating to contracts – negligence, contractual obligations, terms implied in contracts for the sale of goods, hire-purchase, guarantees and indemnities and misrepresentation.

4.1 STANDARD FORMS OF CONTRACT

Key Ideas

Contracts

Businesses are continually dealing with outsiders, and in doing so enter into relationships which are regarded as contracts in law. For example, in the process of setting up, a business may borrow money from outsiders, and buy buildings, plant and equipment. It will then employ labour, and purchase stocks for resale. In the course of time it will make sales and in doing so enter into contracts with customers. Already we have several groups of people with whom contracts will have been formed:

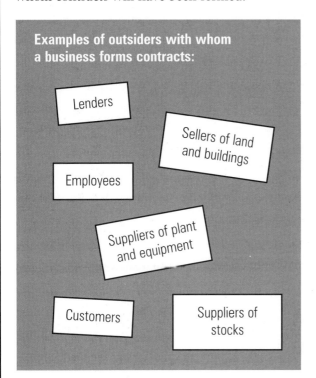

Examples of outsiders with whom a business forms contracts:

Lenders

Sellers of land and buildings

Employees

Suppliers of plant and equipment

Customers

Suppliers of stocks

You can therefore see that a contract is an agreement between two or more parties (e.g. a business and its employees in the case of a Contract of Employment), who promise to give and receive something from each other (consideration) and who intend the contract to be legally binding.

The legal term consideration is used to refer to the promise to give and receive something which is made between the two parties.

There are two main types of contract:

Speciality contracts (also known as contracts by deed or under seal). Here the contract must be in writing and must be 'signed, sealed, and delivered'.

Distinguish Between ...

Simple contracts. These are informal contracts and can be made in any way – by word of mouth, in writing, or simply implied by a person's conduct. For example, when you buy a bag of apples in a shop you are entering into a contract with the seller.

4.1 STANDARD FORMS OF CONTRACT

There are a number of ingredients which are required for an effective contract. These are:

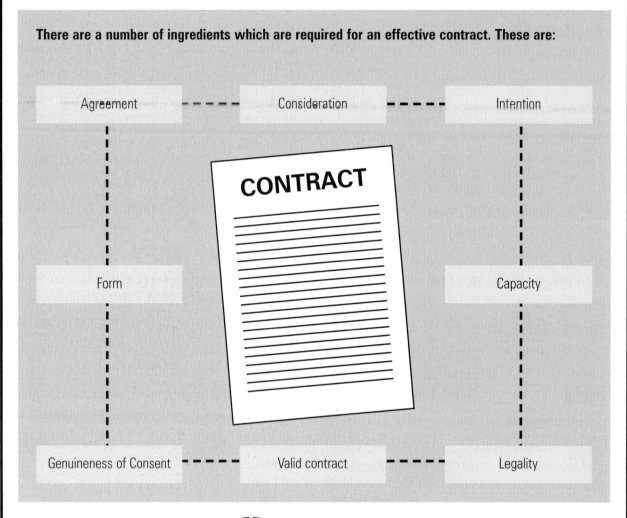

Agreement - - - - Consideration - - - - Intention

Form

Capacity

CONTRACT

Genuineness of Consent - - - - Valid contract - - - - Legality

'That's a deal!'

1   An **agreement** exists in law when one party accepts another's offer. For example, an offer to buy a house at a certain price.

2   **Consideration** involves the two parties showing that their agreement is part of a bargain, i.e. they each promise to give or do something for the other. For example, the seller agrees to sell the house and the buyer agrees to pay for it.

3   The two parties need to **intend** their contract to have legal status. For example, if I promise my wife to cut the grass this morning, we wouldn't see that as a legal contract. However, if we promised to sell our house to a given buyer under agreed terms our intention is to form a legal contract.

4.1 STANDARD FORMS OF CONTRACT

4   In some cases various formalities (**form**) are required such as the completion of specific legal documents, for example a deed of sale.

5   The two parties must be legally capable (**capacity**) of making an agreement. Certain individuals are not regarded to be legally capable because they are too young, too old, too ill, etc.

6   **Genuineness of consent**. The agreement has to be entered into freely and involve a meeting of minds rather than being a forced agreement. For example, where an individual is threatened or misled about the terms of an agreement then they would not have genuinely consented to the agreement.

7   **Legality**. The agreement must be a lawful one. For example, a marriage involving individuals who are too young to marry would not be considered lawful. An agreement made by a company employee to sell off company computers without permission would also be unlawful.

If the above requirements are present then a contract is said to be valid. Should essential elements be missing the contract will then be considered void, voidable or unenforceable.

Doctor Proctor outlines... VOID, VOIDABLE AND UNENFORCEABLE CONTRACTS

The notion of a **void contract** is a contradiction because – if it is void then it is not a contract. A contract is considered to be void if it turns out to be invalid because a mistake has been made and the requirements set out above have not been met. When a contract is declared void then the parties must return (wherever possible) what they have taken from each other, e.g. goods, money, etc.

A **voidable contract** is one that can be made void because there has been some form of misrepresentation or because the contract has been made by someone who does not have the capacity to make one (e.g. someone who is too ill to make a rational decision). Once again measures should be taken to return goods, money, etc. to parties who have mistakenly handed them over to someone else.

An **unenforceable contract** is one which is valid but which can't be enforced in the court because one of the parties refuses to carry out the terms of the contract. Agreements involving the sale of land are unenforceable unless they are set out in writing.

4.1 STANDARD FORMS OF CONTRACT

In recent years there have been many cases where rock stars have sought to void their contracts, because they were often signed when they were little known performers, and were prepared to accept very poor terms. Later they argue that they didn't understand what they were signing at the time.

Sign this and I'll make you a superstar. Trust me, there's no need to read the small print!

Doctor Proctor outlines... THE MAIN TYPES OF BUSINESS CONTRACTS

Business contracts are typically concerned with the following areas:

1. The supply of goods.

The most common form of contract relates to the Sale of Goods, and is dealt with in Unit 5. The Sale of Goods Act defines a contract for the sale of goods as:

'A contract by which the seller transfers or agrees to transfer the property in goods to the buyer for a money consideration called the price.' You can see therefore that the handing over of money is involved as part of the contract.

2. The supply of work and materials

Another form of contract is for the supply of work and materials, e.g. when someone does a repair on your house or motor vehicle.

3. The supply of goods on credit

Because today we live in a credit based economy, there are many rules and regulations and case law dealing with credit transactions.

4. Contracts of bailment

These relate to situations where the owner of goods (the bailor) entrusts the possession of them to another (the bailee), e.g. when a solicitor or bank holds important documents for a business.

5. Employment contracts

These relate to the employment of individuals by a company and are dealt with in Unit 6.

6. Contracts of agency

These are contracts where an organisation or individual employs an agent to work on their behalf when dealing with third parties, e.g. a professional footballer may employ an agent to make contracts on their behalf with a football club and with various sponsors.

7. Contracts concerning land

These include the leasing and mortgaging of land.

8. Financial services contracts

A business uses a range of financial services, e.g. bank loans and insurance. These all involve contracts such as those relating to details of what might be lawfully claimed from an insurance company in relation to the liability of a company to its employees and customers.

4.2 FORMING AN AGREEMENT

Key Ideas 🔑
Offers

An offer is a statement of the terms by which the offeror is prepared to be bound.

There are three components to an agreement:

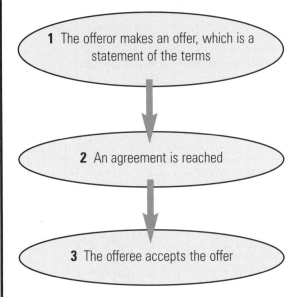

1 The offeror makes an offer, which is a statement of the terms

2 An agreement is reached

3 The offeree accepts the offer

Once these three elements come together in an agreement we have a firm basis for a contract.

The importance of case law

Much of contract law is based on past case law, i.e. on judgments that have been made over time. It is therefore important to examine relevant case examples.

Making an offer is both:

1   A proposal, and

2   A promise to comply with the stated terms.

One of the best known early cases in contract law which is relevant to business agreements was:

Carlill v. *Carbolic Smoke Ball Co.* (1893)

The defendants, the Carbolic Smoke Ball Company, placed advertisements in newspapers stating that they would pay £100 to anybody who caught flu after using one of their smoke balls in the way directed for 14 days. In the adverts they also stated that they had deposited £1,000 with the Alliance Bank to meet any possible claims.

A Mrs Carlill bought one of the smoke balls and used it in the way outlined but still caught the flu. When she tried to claim the £100 she was turned down. She therefore sued Carbolic Smoke Ball Co.

In the court case the defendants claimed that they had attempted to contract with the whole world and that would be impossible. However, the judge held that they had indeed made an offer to the whole world and therefore should be liable to anyone who caught the flu after using their product as set out. Mrs Carlill was able to recover £100. The judge stated that 'if a person chooses to make extravagant promises of this kind he probably does so because it pays him to make them, and, if he has made them, the extravagance of the promises is no reason in law why he should not be bound by them.'

The case highlights the way in which the law recognises offers that have been made to individuals, groups or to the whole world.

4.2 FORMING AN AGREEMENT

Doctor Proctor outlines... 'INVITATION TO TREAT'

When a business organisation makes an offer to sell something it is not always bound in law to accept the first offer made. We use the term 'invitation to treat' to describe a situation where an individual or organisation holds themselves open to offers which they can then accept or reject.

For example, when a company publishes a prospectus inviting people to apply for shares this is an offer to treat – it can choose who to allocate shares to. Similarly, when a mail order company publishes a catalogue advertising goods and stating the terms this is an offer to treat. In the same way goods displayed in a shop window or on a shelf in a supermarket constitute an offer to treat.

At an auction, where furniture or land is being offered – this constitutes an offer to treat and people bid against each other to try and secure the item.

In the case of land sales and house sales – the seller is said to make an offer to treat. This only becomes a definite offer when the terms and conditions are clearly stated.

It is important to be clear therefore whether a business is making an offer or simply making an 'invitation to treat'. In advertising goods it is important for the advertiser to get the wording right so that it is clear which is the case.

In an important case *Pharmaceutical Society of Great Britain* v. *Boots Cash Chemists Ltd* (1953) the Court of Appeal decided that a customer makes an offer when goods are presented for payment at the cash till, and acceptance takes place when the cashier accepts the money (the implication is that the cashier could reject the offer).

An offer

Distinguish Between ...

Intention to make an offer

In the case of *Harvey* v. *Facey* (1893), Harvey sent a telegram asking Facey if he would be prepared to sell Bumper Hall Pen, and if so what would be the lowest price he would accept. Facey replied by telegram stating that this would be at £900. Harvey accepted at this price but Facey refused to sell. The court held that in this case there was no contract because Facey had simply made an offer to treat – if he wanted to sell at some stage £900 would be the lowest price he would accept.

Acceptance

So what constitutes acceptance of an offer?

Once a legal offer has been made, the next step in the agreement is to identify acceptance of that offer. This must take place while the offer is still open, and involve full acceptance.

Case law has established the following rules of acceptance:

1. Acceptance can only be made by the person to whom the offer is made. For example, if I offer to sell a book at a discount only to Pamela Jones, she is the only one that can accept that offer. Obviously this does not relate to an offer made to the world at large as in the Carbolic Smoke Ball case.

2. Acceptance must be absolute and unqualified. In other words the offeree cannot add extra terms and conditions (that requires a new offer). Altering the terms and conditions is referred to as a counter offer. It would then be up to the offeror to make a new offer and have it accepted for acceptance to be absolute and unqualified.

3. Acceptance has to be communicated to the offeror. Typically this will be through word of mouth or written communication. However, the court may deem that the acceptance is implied by the conduct of the acceptor. In the Smoke Ball case Mrs Carlill was not expected by the court to have written back to the Carbolic Smoke Ball Company accepting their offer. The contract is formed at the time and place the acceptance is received by the offeror. If the acceptance is sent by post the contract is formed on posting even if the letter is delayed or lost.

4. Acceptance must be in the mode set out in the offer. For example, an advertisement might ask for an order to be made in writing.

In *Eliason v. Henshaw* (1819). Eliason agreed to buy flour from Henshaw and to pay the waggoner for the flour. However, the acceptance was sent by post and arrived after the waggoner had returned. The court held that there was no contract because the mode set out in the offer had not been employed.

However, more recently courts have ruled that a different mode of acceptance can be considered to form a contract if it does not disadvantage the offeror. This is particularly important for modern business transacted over the Internet and other forms of electronic communications.

Doctor Proctor outlines... SITUATIONS IN WHICH AN OFFER MAY BE TERMINATED

Case law has established a number of situations in which an offer is deemed to be terminated before a contract is formed. These include:

1 Death of either party before acceptance takes place.

2 The passage of an appropriate length of time before acceptance. What is regarded to be appropriate depends on the circumstances –

for example, it would be much shorter for an offer relating to ripe bananas, than for antique furniture.

3 If one party refuses to accept the offer.

4 Where a counter offer is made (i.e. an offer different from the original).

5 If the offeror withdraws or revokes the offer before acceptance.

4.3 Capacity to contract and intention to create legal relations

The law places restrictions on who is able to make contracts. The purpose of restricting the ability to contract is to protect the individuals concerned. For example, there are restrictions on the ability of minors (under 18) and those suffering mental disorder from entering into contracts. Mental disorders relate both to those who are mentally ill and to those temporarily disordered through drink or drugs, who can avoid contracts entered into while they were unaware of events if it can be shown that the other party knew of the incapacity.

Minors enter into contracts on most days of the week, e.g. buying chocolates and CDs, or travelling on a bus. Minors are allowed to make contracts but they are protected from certain types of contract. For example, a minor can be bound in a contract for necessaries (i.e. food, shelter, clothing and education). The definition of necessaries is:

'goods suitable to the condition in life of such a minor, and his actual requirements at the time of sale and delivery.'

Here it must be shown that the goods or services are necessaries, and that as a matter of fact these items are necessaries.

For example, in *Nash* v. *Inman* (1908), where an undergraduate had built up a debt for clothing, the courts held that a minor was not binding in a contract for clothing. He had ordered 11 fancy waistcoats from a tailor, and then refused to pay the bill. The court recognised that clothing is a necessary, and that the clothes would have been suitable for the undergraduate – however, because he already possessed a large quantity of clothes then extra clothes were not a necessary. The message to the tailor given by the court was that he should not try to sell minors clothes that they do not need. It is thus the responsibility of the goods supplier to prove that goods supplied are necessaries. If they are deemed to be necessaries the minor does not necessarily have to pay the contract price but a 'reasonable price'.

Another situation in which a contract is binding on a minor is when there is a 'beneficial contract of service'. In other words the minor will benefit from the contract, e.g. a contract of apprenticeship, education or training.

4.3 CAPACITY TO CONTRACT AND INTENTION TO CREATE LEGAL RELATIONS

There are two categories of minors' contracts:

Binding contracts are ones where the minor must carry out the contract as agreed.

Distinguish Between ...

Voidable contracts do not bind the minor but the other party to the contract is bound. The minor can thus void the contract.

Long-term contracts made by a minor involving shares or land dealings are voidable and can be repudiated by the minor before reaching the age of 18.

Should a minor decide to void a contract then the court can demand when it is 'just and equitable' for property and other items to be returned, e.g. the waistcoats in the *Nash* v. *Inman* case.

Where a minor repudiates a contract that has already been partially met then the other party can fairly claim for the benefit that the minor has thus far received. For example, if a minor was buying on credit an electronic speaker system which they did not need and had already had the item for three months, then they might be expected to pay for that three months for the benefit already received.

In the case of mental patients, contracts made during periods in which they are lucid are regarded to be binding, but not when they are not fully in control of their senses.

In Unit 3 we looked at the capacity of Partnerships and Companies to engage in contracts. We showed that Directors and Partners can engage in contracts providing it is within their powers to do so in the Articles or Partnership Agreement.

4.3 CAPACITY TO CONTRACT AND INTENTION TO CREATE LEGAL RELATIONS

Key Ideas 🔑

Intention to create legal relations

If I regularly give my children pocket money my intention is not to create a legal relation. However, if I agree to pay my window cleaner £10 every time she cleans my windows this is a legal relationship.

In addition to individuals engaging in contracts having the capacity to contract, it is also a necessary requirement for a contract for the parties to have the intention of being legally bound.

Case law has established that:

1. In **social and domestic agreements** there is no intention to be legally bound. For example, in *Balfour* v. *Balfour* (1919), the defendant was a civil servant working in Sri Lanka. When he went back he left his wife in England for health reasons and he agreed to send her £30 a month. Later they divorced and he stopped paying her. The court decreed that in cases where husband and wife made arrangements between themselves, the parties did not intend this to form a legal arrangement.

However, this is not a rule. Where the court sees fit it may regard the arrangement to be legally binding.

2. In contrast, **commercial agreements** are regarded to be legally binding and are assumed to be intended to create legal relations. However, if in the wording to such an agreement it is stated 'this is not intended to be a legal agreement' then in law this is not regarded as being intended to create legal arrangements.

4.4 CONSIDERATION

Key Ideas

Exchange

Consideration is the process of exchange in a bargain – one party agrees to do one thing for the other and this benefit is reciprocated. An example of a simple exchange involves paying money to a shopkeeper to receive goods.

An example of executed consideration would be:

Promise: A national magazine says that it will give a £5,000 prize for the best student essay it receives about changes in the law in Britain.

Act: Sumaya Patel is judged by a panel to have written the best student essay, and as a result receives the prize.

A good way of thinking about consideration from the point of view of the parties concerned is that it is what they expect to get out of a bargain that they have entered into. If they don't get this consideration then they might want to take the case to the courts.

These are the two main types of consideration.

Executed consideration involves one party promising to do something in exchange for the act of another.

An example of executory consideration would be:

Promise: The Law Society promises to sponsor the student essay prize competition next year.

Promise: The national magazine promises to place a free advertisement for the Law Society in its pages the next year.

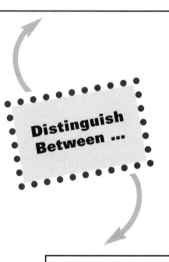

Distinguish Between ...

Executory consideration involves promises by at least two parties to perform acts that benefit each other in the future.

4.4 CONSIDERATION

The following ingredients are regarded to be necessary for consideration to be considered as having value.

1. Value and adequacy. The courts are only concerned that parties to the bargain receive what they were offered when the bargain was struck. If they receive this then it is felt to be adequate. For example, in the case of *Chappell and Co. Ltd* v. *Nestlés Co. Ltd* (1960), the wrappers of three bars of chocolate were considered to be adequate value as consideration in a deal where the wrappers and 1s 6d formed the price paid for a copy of a record called 'Rockin' Shoes'.

2. Consideration must not be in the past. Consideration does not relate to the past. For example, in a case *Roscorla* v. *Thomas* (1842), the two parties made an agreement to exchange a horse (consideration) for a sum of money (consideration). As the horse was being led away the purchaser asked if the horse was vicious. The seller told him that it wasn't – and if it was he would repay the money. In the event the horse proved to be vicious but the court held that the buyer had bought the horse before the second promise of the seller and so the consideration (the promise to pay back the money) could not be applied to the earlier agreement.

3. Promises involving debts. Promises to pay smaller sums to be released from paying a large sum which is owed is not regarded to be good consideration.

4. The promise must be more than a duty. If a Premier League goalkeeper promised that he would try to stop goals going in if he was given a bonus this would not be considered to be good consideration. This is because it is already his duty to stop goals and he is being paid to do just that. However, if he agreed to wash the team's kit for payment after each match this would be considered as good consideration because he would be paid for something that is not in his normal contract.

5. The position of third parties
A plaintiff bringing an action in court must show that he or she made a promise of consideration. If my next door neighbour promises a delivery firm that I will pay for a delivery to be made to my house, the delivery firm will not be able to enforce the contract on me because I have not given consideration for the promise my neighbour made. Consideration relates to the parties involved directly in making an agreement.

4.5 ILLEGALITY

Key Ideas 🔑

Legality

In law a court action cannot arise from an illegal act. So if a contract requires one or both parties to do something illegal then it is not a lawful contract.

A contract is considered to be illegal if:

1 It involves an act that directly breaks the law – for example, I make a contract with you to buy stolen property from you.

2 It involves an act that is harmful to public policy.

Where a contract is illegal right from the start it will be considered void and thus be unenforceable. Generally speaking money or goods transferred under the contract will not be able to be reclaimed, but there are exceptions, where one of the parties innocently took up the contract not realising that illegal acts were taking place. The innocent party can protect their rights providing they immediately put a stop to the contract.

Contracts in restraint of trade

Typically the law in this country encourages free and fair competition between businesses. As a result, over the years a number of cases have provided precedents in common law which give the courts powers against the restraint of trade. A contract which is in restraint of trade is held to be contrary to public policy and will be void unless it can be shown to be reasonable.

Examples of contracts in restraint of trade include:

(Note: Doctor Proctor says that if these restraints are considered by the courts to be 'reasonable' then the restraint is acceptable.)

1 Terms in contracts which restrict an employee's freedom to work once the contract is ended. For example, part of a contract that states that an author of a book will not write a book for any other publisher after completing a publishing contract with the existing publisher.

Doctor Proctor outlines... EXAMPLES OF CONTRACTS WHICH ARE ILLEGAL BECAUSE THEY ARE HARMFUL TO PUBLIC POLICY

There are a number of situations in which contracts will be declared illegal because they are harmful to public policy, including:

1 Contracts that are illegal at common law – for example, contracting an accountant to fiddle the books being presented to the Inland Revenue.

2 Contracts encouraging corruption in public life – for example, contracting with a local government officer to favour a company in awarding business contracts.

3 Contracts trading with an enemy during wartime or to supply businesses in a country where there is a legal embargo such as the embargo on military contracts with Iraq.

4.5 ILLEGALITY

2 A sales agreement by which a trader agrees to buy from only one supplier.

3 A contract for the sale of a business whereby the seller agrees not to compete with the buyer. For example, if one undertaker buys the funeral business of another undertaker he or she may put a term in the contract stopping the original undertaker from setting up a new business in the neighbourhood. The court may consider this to be unreasonable if it is against the public interest.

4 Contracts between businesses to restrict prices and outputs. These aspects are governed by the Restrictive Trade Practices Acts 1976 and 1977 and Resale Price Act 1976. These Acts have encouraged price competition because suppliers are not able to control the prices charged by retail and other outlets. Most recently we have seen increasing competition over book prices, and Internet booksellers are able to discount the price of books rather than being controlled by publishers.

So as well as common law discouraging the restraint of trade there are specific Acts of Parliament like the Resale Price Act supporting competition.

Reality of consent

A contract which is regular in all ways may still not be regarded to be valid because there is no real consent to it by one or both of the parties. There is no consensus ad idem or meeting of the minds. Consent may be rendered unreal by mistake, misrepresentation, or duress and undue influence.

Mistake

Mistake does not generally make a contract unavoidable unless a real agreement between the parties was never formed. In an interesting case, *Raffles* v. *Wichelhaus* (1864), the buyer had agreed to purchase cotton sailing on the SS Peerless from Bombay. However, what neither of the parties to the contract knew was that there were two ships called SS Peerless sailing in different months. The buyer thought that he had bought cotton sailing on the first ship, whereas the seller thought he had sold cotton on the second ship. Because of this mistake the contract was not upheld.

If a party to a contract knows all the relevant facts then his or her bad judgment is not considered to be a mistake.

Typical mistakes are:

1 Mistakes about the subject matter of the contract as, for example, in the case outlined above (*Raffles* v. *Wichelhaus*).

2 Mistakenly signing a contract in the belief that a document of a different nature is being signed. Originally the defence of non est factum ('it is not my deed') was introduced to protect those who couldn't read who had signed deeds which had been incorrectly read over to them.

3   Mistakes where one party is mistaken about the identity of the other party, e.g. when Jones contracts with Bill Smith thinking that he is contracting with William Smith. In most cases these involve some element of fraud and are fairly easy to prove.

4   Unconscionable bargains. Where one party exploits a weakness in the other, e.g. where a buyer manages to buy an item off an elderly person at a price well below the market value. In *Clifford Davis Management* v. *WEA Records* (1975), an experienced music industry manager obtained a contract with a pop star who had little or no business experience, under which the recording artist gave the manager the copyright in all his compositions for a period of years. The court held that the pop star could avoid the contract because of his inferior bargaining position.

Misrepresentation

The term misrepresentation is used to describe a situation in which there is no genuineness of consent to a contract by one of the parties. The effect on the contract is less serious because the contract becomes voidable rather than void. The injured party can then ask the court to put them back in the position they were in before the contract was made.

A **representation** is an inducement to make a contract. It is a statement of some specific existing and verifiable fact or past event. It becomes a misrepresentation when it is false. A **misrepresentation** therefore is a false statement of facts or past events.

Distinguish Between ...

In law, misrepresentations must be distinguished from manufacturers' and sellers' boasts or 'puffs'. For example, if a local garage states 'we give you the best deals in town' that is just a puff. However, if the garage claims 'all of the cars we sell are brand new' whereas in fact they are second-hand this is misrepresentation.

Today we use the term 'hype' to describe what is quaintly termed a 'puff'.

The main types of misrepresentation are:

1   **Fraud**

     Where a false statement is made:

     •   knowingly, or

     •   without belief in its truth, or

     •   recklessly, not caring whether true or false.

2   **Innocent**

     Where a false statement was made unknowingly.

3   **Negligent**

     Where a false statement is made where the maker did not have reasonable grounds for believing the statement to be true.

4.6 DURESS AND UNDUE INFLUENCE

Key Ideas 🔑

Duress

The legal concept of **duress** means actual violence or threats of violence to the person or the contracting party or those near and dear to him or her. These threats must be calculated to produce fear of loss of life or bodily harm.

In practice it is more common for contracts to be formed by threats of violence than by threats of loss of life.

In some cases the courts judge that duress makes a contract voidable whereas in others that it makes a contract void. This issue is important to third parties. For example, if Smith gains goods from Jones by duress and then sells them on to Brown, who is not aware of the duress – then Jones will be able to recover the goods from Brown if the contract is void, but not if it is voidable.

Economic duress
In recent years the courts have also developed the concept of economic duress where one party, because of its sheer size, power, and influence, is able to put undue pressure on a smaller concern or individual. The court protects small companies and individuals against such duress.

Undue influence

The legal concept of **undue influence** deals with contracts or gifts obtained without free consent by the influence of one mind over another.

The party seeking to avoid the contract must show that the other had undue influence over them. The party seeking to enforce the contract must show that undue influence was not used, i.e. that the contract was made by a free and independent mind.

There are a number of situations in which confidential or fiduciary interests exist between parties, e.g. parent and child, solicitor and client, trustee and beneficiary, guardian and ward, etc. where undue influence may be exerted. The facts of a case must be such that they show that undue influence was exerted.

4.7 EXCLUSION CLAUSES

Key Ideas

Small print

Exclusion clauses often present one of the nastier sides of contract law. They are usually presented in the small print of a contract. They come into play when someone who believes that they have a contract of a certain nature suddenly finds there are various exclusion clauses that appear to exclude the other party from meeting the contract in the way expected.

Although exclusion clauses are allowed, both the courts and Parliament are reluctant to allow exclusion clauses to operate where they are imposed on a weaker party such as an ordinary consumer, by a stronger party such as a large high street discount store.

Typically the courts will protect the consumer by:

1 Stating that the exclusion clauses were not part of the contract.

2 Interpreting the contract so as to prevent the application of the exclusion clause/s.

Doctor Proctor outlines... KEY FEATURES OF THE LAW RELATING TO EXCLUSION CLAUSES

- The party seeking to enforce the exclusion clause will need to show that the other party agreed to the clause when the contract was made.

- If the clause is part of a written document, then the signer is usually bound to what they have signed even if they have not read it, unless misrepresentation took place.

- If the clause is not part of a written document then the person seeking to rely on the exclusion clause will need to be able to show that attention had been drawn to the clause.

- Any attempt to introduce an exclusion clause after a contract has been made is ineffective because the consideration for the clause is past.

- An exclusion clause may be made ineffective by an inconsistent oral promise. For example, if one thing is written in the small print of a contract, and another understanding is communicated orally then the small print is not held as being an acceptable exclusion.

- If there is ambiguity or reason for doubt about the meaning of an exclusion clause, the courts will view it in a way that is unfavourable to the party that drew up the exclusion clause.

- What is known as the 'repugnancy rule' sets out that if the exemption clause is in direct contradiction to the purposes of the contract then the clause can be struck out.

- If a party to a contract does something which is fundamentally against what they have contracted to do then an exclusion clause will not protect them.

4.8 EXPRESS AND IMPLIED TERMS

The **express terms** of a contract involve what was said or written in relation to what each of the parties to a contract intend to do in order to undertake their part of the contract.

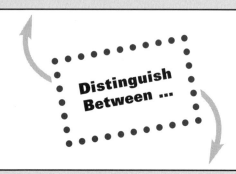

In cases involving contracts it is necessary to consider what was said by the parties concerned and the extent to which this can be considered a contract.

Prior to a contract being made, representations will be made of various facts and information that are relevant to a contract. If these are false then misrepresentation will have occurred as discussed earlier (4.5). In the creation of the contract itself various terms will be specified and these can be broken down into two main types – express and implied terms.

The courts will seek to implement the intentions of the contracting parties as they appear from the statements that they make.

When the statement is such that a party to the contract would not have made the contract without it, then it should be considered a term of the statement.

In any contract, some of the terms are going to be more important to the overall contract than others. The law therefore distinguishes between:

Conditions are the fundamental obligations set out in a contract.

Warranties are less important (subsidiary) obligations; a failure to perform these does not undermine the roots of the contract. (Note that this use of the term warranty is different from the more familiar one of a guarantee.)

Doctor Proctor outlines... THE STATUS OF DIFFERENT TYPES OF STATEMENTS

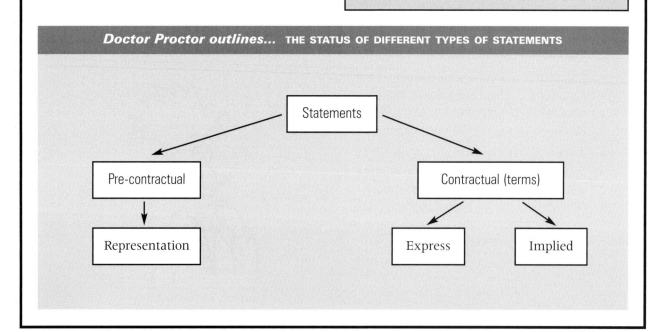

4.8 EXPRESS AND IMPLIED TERMS

In addition to the express terms set out by the parties, a contract may also contain and be subject to implied terms. These terms arise from custom or statute, and in addition implied terms may be implied by the court to achieve what the court views as the original intentions of the parties. For example, if by custom and practice a firm has typically received goods of a given quality standard from its supplier, it would be assumed that a new contract to supply, say, apples would also imply a similar level of quality.

In addition to customary terms, a judge may also imply a term into a contract because he or she sees it as enabling the express terms of the contract to meet the original intentions of the parties.

Finally, the implied terms of a contract are assumed to be those that comply with statutory requirements even though these may not be stated in a written or oral contract.

All implied terms must comply with statutory requirements if they are to be considered lawful

4.9 TERMINATION OF A CONTRACT

There are four main ways in which a contract can be discharged (terminated).

2. By performance

1. By agreement

Discharge of contracts

3. Frustration

4. Breach

1. By agreement

In creating an agreement the parties may agree a point at which it will be terminated, e.g. a Premier League player is contracted to play for the club for a two year period. Generally, in such contracts there would be terms allowing termination by notice. There are usually statutory requirements relating to the amount of notice that should be given.

A contract can also be terminated by the creation of a new agreement, which must include consideration. If neither party has yet kept their side of the original agreement then this is easy, because the consideration is the fact that each of the parties waives their rights. However, if one party has not kept their side of the agreement then typically they will have to provide fresh consideration.

2. By performance

Performance involves parties to the contract performing their part of the bargain, e.g. to supply materials and to be paid for them.

There are varying levels of performance that are acceptable to the court as illustrated below:

i) Complete performance – where every term and warranty has been discharged.

ii) Substantial performance – where the court is of the opinion that the contract is substantially performed it may allow one or both parties to make recovery for minor details not fully completed. For substantial performance to be discharged the court would make a distinction between conditions and warranties – with the conditions needing to be discharged for substantial perforamance.

iii) Acceptance of partial performance. If a party accepts an element of partial performance, e.g. paying for 100 books when 200 had been ordered, then they will only be able to make a claim on the further 100 undelivered books.

3. Frustration

If it is impossible to perform a contract from the outset then it is void. For example, if a bookseller agreed to supply a book but then found that it was no longer available from the publisher, or if a farmer agreed to sell a crop that was destroyed by weather conditions.

Contracts of personal service are discharged by the death of a party who was to perform the service.

The principle of frustration will usually apply where there is no fault by either of the parties.

4. Breach of contract

Breach occurs when a party to the contract fails to discharge their part of the contract lawfully. Breach typically fits into two categories – anticipatory and actual breach.

Anticipatory breach takes place when breach occurs before the time for performance to arrive. The wronged party can immediately sue for damages or wait until the time when the performance is expected to occur.

Distinguish Between ...

Actual breach involves breach in the performance of contractual terms.

It is necessary for the innocent party to show that the breach affects a vital part of the contract, i.e. a condition rather than a warranty.

4.10 ARBITRATION

Arbitrator

Many commercial contracts contain a provision whereby the parties agree to put disputes before an arbitrator. In some instances the arbitrator may be a trained lawyer but this need not be the case. Most importantly the arbitrator needs to be someone with knowledge and experience of the relevant area, e.g. a surveyor in a building dispute.

Arbitration is a good way of resolving contractual disputes in private rather than going to the courts where a legal report would be published which could be picked up as a headline story in the national press.

Doctor Proctor outlines... THE NATURE OF ARBITRATION PROCEEDINGS

Arbitration proceedings differ from those that take place in a court:

1   They are carried out in private, and the outcome may not be publicised.

2   The arbitrator has specialist knowledge whereas a judge is unlikely to have any.

Parties typically choose arbitration because they do not want to have the case publicised, perhaps because it would be bad for the company name and for business in general.

Arbitration is not necessarily a cheap process because the arbitrator may charge £1,000 or more a day, and lawyers charge the same fees as they would in a court case.

These cases may also be long and drawn out because the parties may not agree on the findings, and they may spend a long time agreeing on an arbitrator who would be acceptable to all parties.

Arbitration must take account of the various statutory requirements such as the Unfair Terms in Consumer Contracts Regulations Act 1994 which does not allow businesses to apply unfair contract terms. The Arbitration Act 1996 applies these regulations to arbitration clauses – so that an unfair clause cannot be enforced in an Arbitration proceeding. If this is the case a consumer could use the civil courts to apply for damages.

4.11 REMEDIES

> ### Key Ideas 🔑
>
> ### Damages

Remedies are what the injured party in a contract is entitled to in order to try and put right the injury they have suffered. A breach of contract gives the injured party the right in common law to seek to recover the damages (i.e. financial compensation). Other forms of remedy include specific performance and injunction.

Damages

Sometimes the parties to a contract are able to foresee the possibility of the contract breaking down and therefore set out how much damages need to be paid should this happen.

Unliquidated damages are not decided beforehand but are designed to put the injured party in the position he or she would have been in if the contract had been carried out properly.

Distinguish Between ...

Liquidated damages are ones that are decided at the time of making a contract and should be based on a genuine estimation of the damage. For example, when buying a holiday from a travel firm, your entitlement to compensation may be part of the contract.

Penalty clauses – are often inserted in a contract to ensure that the contract is performed properly, they are not necessarily a reflection of damage.

Doctor Proctor outlines... ASSESSMENT OF UNLIQUIDATED DAMAGES

Unliquidated damages are designed as compensation for loss rather than as a punishment. So for example, if a seller fails to deliver goods, but the buyer is able to buy elsewhere at no extra cost then the claimant would only be able to receive nominal damages – e.g. a sum of £5.

Examples of the sorts of things that businesses might have to pay damages for include compensation for financial loss, personal injury and damage to property. In addition, compensation may be given for disappointment and mental distress.

4.11 REMEDIES

In deciding whether to grant damages the courts need to know where to draw the line. Courts therefore are interested in what is termed 'remoteness of damages'. The law relating to remoteness of damages is based on a case:

Hadley v. *Baxendale* (1854)

In this case the plaintiff owned a mill and had ordered a piece of machinery to be delivered by a given date. The carrier (Baxendale) was late in delivery and Hadley sued for loss of profits during the period that the machinery was not in operation. The court judged that the damages were too remote because Baxendale didn't realise that the delay stopped the mill from working. The court set out that damages should be awarded where:

1   They arise naturally from a contract.

2   They are reasonably in the contemplation of both parties at the time when they entered into the contract, as the probable result of breach of the contract.

In a further case, *Victoria Laundry* v. *Newman Industries Ltd* (1948), where a boiler for Victoria Laundry was supplied five months late, the court decided that damages should include:

•   The normal profits of the laundry because the supplier knew that the laundry needed the boiler for its normal production.

But not:

•   The special dyeing profits that the business might make, because the supplier was not aware of these contracts at the time of making the contract.

Doctor Proctor outlines... EQUITABLE REMEDIES

Equitable remedies

In addition to common law remedies there are two other forms of remedy which have developed in equity.

1. Specific performance

This is an order by the court requiring the party that is in breach of a contract to carry out his or her contractual obligations. Failure to do so may give rise to penalties for contempt of court.

This remedy may not be used in the following circumstances:

1. When damages are an adequate remedy. Most breaches of contract can be remedied through the award of financial compensation.

2. Equity requires mutuality in terms of remedies – i.e. both parties must be able to ask the court to impose specific performance. In some cases this is not possible, e.g. when either party is a minor.

3. An order will not be made unless the court is in a position to supervise its enforcement. For example, this remedy would not be used in the case of building contracts because the court could not supervise them on an ongoing basis.

4. The courts have discretion to refuse specific performance in other cases as appropriate.

2. Injunction

An injunction is a remedy that a court can impose to stop a party from breaking a contract. It is not used in situations where damages provide an adequate solution, but will be used to restrain a breach of contract for personal services. A well known example of this is in the case of *Warner Bros* v. *Nelson* (1937) where the actress Bette Davis had an exclusive film contract. The court stopped her from making a film with another company.

Recission

We use the term recission to apply to the equitable remedy of placing parties back in the position they were in before a contract was made – e.g. by returning goods and money back to their original owners.

4.12 THE MISREPRESENTATION ACT 1967

Key Ideas

Non-fraudulent misrepresentation

The Misrepresentation Act 1967 marked an important milestone in providing protection for people who had entered into contracts. In particular it clarified the position of the courts in relation to non-fraudulent misrepresentation including negligent and unknowing misrepresentation.

Until the passing of the Misrepresentation Act the courts did not have general powers to award damages in cases of non-fraudulent misrepresentation.

In 1967 the Act changed this requirement. It reads:

'When a person has entered into a contract after a misrepresentation has been made to him by another party thereto and as a result thereof he has suffered loss then if the person making the representation would be liable in damages in respect thereof had the representation been made fraudulently, that person shall be so liable notwithstanding that the misrepresentation was not made fraudulently, unless he proves that he had reasonable grounds to believe and did believe up to the time that the contract was made that the facts represented were true'.

Other key features of the Act were that:

In cases of negligent misrepresentation (i.e. where the person making the statement has no reason to believe that it is true) injured parties are more likely to be successful under the Act, because it reverses the normal burden of proof. The defendant will only escape liability if they can prove that they made the statement innocently.

If misrepresentation is neither fraudulent nor negligent, the only possible remedy is recission.

A clause excluding liability for misrepresentation or cutting down an individual's remedies for misrepresentation is only valid if it satisfies the test of 'reasonableness'.

The Act makes it clear that an innocent party will have remedies for misrepresentation even though the representation has become a term of contract.

4.13 THE UNFAIR CONTRACT TERMS ACT 1977

Key Ideas 🔑

Unfair terms

The Unfair Contract Terms Act 1977 sought to prevent unfair terms in contracts particularly relating to exclusion clauses. In particular the Act gives protection to consumers, although the same principles apply to business contracts.

Reasonableness

The courts will uphold clauses which are considered to be reasonable. It is up to the party entering the clause into a contract to prove that it is reasonable.

There are various considerations that the courts bear in mind when deciding whether a clause is reasonable including:

Where the clause limits the amount payable – this will in some measure be determined by the means available to make such a payment, and the extent to which it is possible to take insurance cover.

Where the contract is for the supply of goods –

- the relative bargaining strength of the parties concerned;

- the availability of other suppliers;

- inducement to agree to the clause;

- buyer's knowledge of the extent of the clause;

- customs of trade and previous dealings.

Doctor Proctor outlines... CLAUSES THAT ARE NOT ACCEPTABLE UNDER THE ACT

There are a number of clauses that are rendered ineffective by the Act including:

1 If a trader uses an exclusion clause to avoid liability for death or personal injury caused by negligence, that clause is always unenforceable, whether in a contract term or on a notice.

2 A manufacturer's guarantee cannot exclude or restrict that manufacturer's liability for loss or damage arising from defect in goods when used by a consumer which results from negligence in manufacture or distribution.

3 Other clauses where traders unfairly seek to escape their responsibilities under a contract.

4.14 THE UNFAIR TERMS IN CONSUMER CONTRACTS REGULATIONS 1999

Key Ideas

Unfair terms

Unfair terms are ones which cause a significant imbalance in the rights and obligations of the parties under the contract, to the detriment of the consumer.

Example

Examples of unfair terms are:

'No responsibility for loss or damage to garments, however caused' on the back of a dry-cleaning ticket is an example of an unfair exclusion clause.

Four examples from the small print are:

- Stopping you holding back part of the price of services, if they turn out to be faulty.

- Preventing you (but not the trader) from withdrawing from the contract.

- Allowing the trader not to honour promises made.

- Stopping you from being able to go to court.

The Regulations implement the EC Directive on Unfair Terms in Consumer Contracts. They apply to any term in a contract between a seller or supplier who is acting for business purposes and a consumer (not a company) who is acting for purposes outside of business where the term has not been individually negotiated. Typically these relate to pre-printed contract terms, although they do apply to oral terms.

An unfair term is not binding on the consumer but the contract will continue to bind the parties if it is viable without the unfair term. An example of an unfair term that was not binding was when a mobile phone company demanded that a customer should pay call charges even after the customer had informed the company that their mobile phone had been stolen.

Standard form contracts presented to consumers must be in easy to understand English if they are to be valid. If there is any doubt about the meaning of a term, the meaning which is most favourable to the consumer will apply.

The Director General of Fair Trading is responsible for considering complaints and can apply to the courts for an injunction against persons recommending or using unfair terms.

Section 4.1: Standard forms of contract

1 Describe two ways that a simple contract can be made.

2 When does an agreement exist in law?

3 What is meant by genuineness of consent?

4 Why is the term 'void contract' a contradiction?

5 What is an unenforceable contract?

6 List four purposes for which a contract might be made.

Section 4.2: Forming an agreement

1 Why was Mrs Carlill able to retrieve £100 from the Carbolic Smoke Ball Co?

2 What is an 'invitation to treat'?

3 What is meant by acceptance?

4 Explain why:

a) Jones cannot accept an offer made by Smith to Brown?

b) In some circumstances I might not be able to accept an offer by sending an e-mail.

Section 4.3: Capacity to contract and intention to create legal relations

1 Can minors enter into contracts?

2 Why should a shopkeeper watch out when selling expensive clothes to minors on credit terms?

3 Which are more binding and why – social and domestic agreements or commercial agreements?

Section 4.4: Consideration

1 If I agree to give you £5 does this involve consideration?

2 Why were the wrappers of three bars of chocolate accepted as consideration by the courts in the case of *Chappell and Co. Ltd* v. *Nestlés Co. Ltd* (1960)?

3 If a teacher promises to mark students' work should this be accepted as consideration for them paying him £10?

Section 4.5: Illegality

1 Under what circumstances would a contract be considered illegal?

2 Give two examples of illegal contracts which would be in restraint of trade.

3 Does a mistake make a contract unavoidable?

4 Give one example of a mistake.

5 What is a puff? Would a puff be considered as misrepresentation?

Section 4.6: Duress and undue influence

1 What is normally meant by duress?

2 What is economic duress?

3 What is meant by undue influence?

Section 4.7: Exclusion clauses

1 If there is ambiguity in an exclusion clause who will the court favour?

2 If an exclusion clause is not part of a written document how will the person seeking to enforce it try to build up their case?

3 What is the 'repugnancy rule' with regard to exclusion clauses?

Section 4.8: Express and implied terms

1 What is an implied term?

2 How would a party to a contract know about express terms?

3 What is the difference between a condition and a warranty in a contract?

Section 4.9: Termination of a contract

1 What is the difference between termination by agreement and termination by performance?

2 What is complete performance?

3 Explain what is meant by frustration.

4 What is meant by breach of contract?

Section 4.10: Arbitration

1 Why might parties to an agreement prefer arbitration rather than going to the courts to solve a dispute?

2 Why is arbitration a costly business?

Section 4.11: Remedies

1 What are damages?

2 What are a) liquidated damages and b) penalties?

3 Why is an injunction considered to be a remedy?

Section 4.12: The Misrepresentation Act 1967

1 What was the major change made by this Act?

2 What is the position if a misrepresentation is set out as a term of a contract?

Section 4.13: The Unfair Contract Terms Act 1977

1 What is meant by the term reasonableness?

2 List two considerations of reasonableness in relation to the supply of goods.

Section 4.14: The Unfair Terms in Consumer Contracts Regulations 1999

1 What is an unfair term in a consumer contract?

2 Give an example of an unfair term.

3 Is an unfair term binding on a consumer?

UNIT 5

CONSUMER PROTECTION LEGISLATION

Topics covered in this unit

5.1 Sale of Goods Act 1979 (amended by the Sale and Supply of Goods Act 1994)

These Acts cover most goods and services that we purchase and we have certain rights under these acts. Goods should be 'as described', 'of satisfactory quality' and 'fit for purpose'. When you buy a service you can expect it to be carried out 'using reasonable care and skill', 'within a reasonable time' and 'at a reasonable charge'.

5.2 Supply of Goods and Services Act 1982

This Act relates to the supply of goods and services together, for example when a firm has a maintenance contract to maintain a central heating system for a customer. As part of the contract they will supply goods, parts and labour.

5.3 Sale and Supply of Goods to Consumers Regulations 2002

These implement the EU Directive of 1999 and build on existing UK consumer protection law. The main changes are that for the first six months after purchase/delivery, the burden of proof when reporting faulty goods is reversed in the consumer's favour. In addition guarantees offered by manufacturers or retailers must be legally binding and written in plain English.

5.4 Consumer Protection Act 1987

This Act established that the producer of defective goods is primarily liable for damage caused by such goods.

5.5 Trade Descriptions Act 1968

This Act makes it a criminal offence for a trader to describe goods falsely. Breaking the Trade Descriptions Act is a criminal offence.

5.6 Weights and Measures Act 1985

This Act aims to ensure that consumers receive the actual quantity or weight of a product that they believe they are buying.

Topics covered in this unit

5.7 Consumer Credit Act 1974

The Consumer Credit Act covers a range of 'regulated' agreements where credit is defined as a 'cash loan or any other form of financial accommodation'. The Act sets out the rights and responsibilities of parties involved in credit agreements.

5.8 Data Protection Act 1998

The Data Protection Act sets out a legal framework to regulate the use of computers in the processing of personal information. The Data Protection Registrar is responsible for keeping a public register of those involved in processing personal information.

5.9 Environment Act 1995

European Union Regulations and increasing concern for the environment have led to a flood of new laws in this country such as the Environment Act and the Pollution Prevention and Control regulations.

5.10 The Small Claims Court and the County Court

The **small claims court** and the **county court** exist to resolve contractual disputes between parties including those relating to consumer protection.

5.1 SALE OF GOODS ACT 1979 (AMENDED BY THE SALE AND SUPPLY OF GOODS ACT 1994)

Key Ideas 🔑

Fit for the purpose

These two Acts provide an important framework of protection for consumers of goods and services.

These requirements relate to any sort of trader (e.g. shop, street market, mail order, or door-to-door salesperson), and any goods you buy from these traders should meet these basic requirements. They also apply to food and goods bought in sales.

If there is something wrong with a good or service the buyer should tell the seller as soon as possible. Taking faulty goods back straight away should entitle the buyer to getting their money back. They have not legally 'accepted' the goods, and this means that they can 'reject' them. The consumer can still reject goods even if they have taken them home.

Doctor Proctor explains... HOW THESE ACTS RELATE TO THE BUYING OF GOODS

The Acts set out that goods must be:

- 'Of satisfactory quality' – i.e. free from significant faults, except defects that are drawn to the buyer's attention by the seller (for instance, if goods are declared to be 'shop-soiled').

- 'Fit for the purpose' – including any particular purpose mentioned by the customer to the seller. For example, if the customer asks for a jumper that is machine-washable, they would not expect to be sold one that has to be only hand washed.

- 'As described' – i.e. on the package or sales literature, or verbally by the seller. If the customer is told that a shirt is 100% cotton, then it should not turn out to be a mixture of cotton and polyester.

5.1 SALE OF GOODS ACT 1979 (AMENDED BY THE SALE AND SUPPLY OF GOODS ACT 1994)

Doctor Proctor explains... HOW THESE LAWS RELATE TO BUYING A SERVICE

When a customer pays for a service – for example, from a dry cleaner, travel agent, car mechanic, hairdresser or builder – they are entitled to certain standards.

A service should be carried out:

- Within a reasonable time. If the customer has their hi-fi system repaired, it should not take weeks and weeks. The customer can agree on a definite completion time with the supplier of the service.

- With reasonable care and skill. The job should be done to a proper standard of workmanship. For example, if a customer has a dress made for a special occasion, it should not fray or come apart at the seams for no reason.

- At a reasonable charge, if no price has been fixed in advance. However, if the price is fixed at the outset or some other way has been used to work out the charge, then the customer can't complain later that it was unreasonable.

The Sale of Goods Act is based on the assumption that there are a number of implied terms involved 'where the seller sells goods in the course of their business'. For example, there is an implied condition that the goods supplied under the contract are of a satisfactory quality and are fit for the purpose.

Fitness for purpose in terms of *Jewson Ltd* v. *Kelly* (2002).

In this case, the claimant ('Jewson') brought an action for £55,322.43 for the sale and delivery of 12 electric boilers supplied to the defendant. The defendant argued that the boilers were not fit for the particular purpose for which Jewson knew that they were required and counterclaimed for the substantial losses he claimed to have suffered as a result.

Kelly argued that the boilers had a very low SAP rating (a rating which gives guidance on the energy efficiency of the heating system in a domestic property).

The court concluded that an unacceptable SAP rating would substantially increase the risk that a proposed sale of a property would be delayed significantly or even abandoned. Although there was no intrinsic defect in the boilers, the Court concluded that they were not of satisfactory quality.

5.2 SUPPLY OF GOODS AND SERVICES ACT 1982

Key Ideas

Supply contracts

The supply of goods and services relates to contracts for work and material, for example, the repair of your central heating system, where goods and services are supplied together.

Supply of goods – a new boiler.

Supply of services – fitting of the boiler and repair of the central heating.

In relation to contracts for work and materials:

- The supply of goods (or the materials used) is covered by part 1 of the Supply of Goods and Services Act.

- The supply of services is covered by part 2 of the Act.

Contracts in part 1 for the transfer of goods relate to contracts under which one person transfers, or agrees to transfer to another, the property in goods. There must be a contract between the two parties.

Contracts for work and materials include:

1 Maintenance contracts, where a firm contracts to maintain something, e.g. a set of computers, by providing labour and spare parts.

2 Building and construction contracts where the builder supplies labour and materials.

3 Installation and improvement contracts, e.g. by installing furniture into a building or painting the interior.

Doctor Proctor outlines... THE TERMS IMPLIED IN CONTRACTS FOR THE TRANSFER OF GOODS, WORK AND MATERIALS

There are a number of terms implied in contracts for the supply of goods and services.

These include:

1 **Title**. That the supplier has a right to transfer the property in the goods to the customer.

2 **Description**. That the goods will be as described.

3 **Satisfactory quality**. The goods must be fit for the purpose that they are supplied for.

4 **Sample**. If the work is sold on the basis of a sample then it is expected that the rest of the work will correspond to the sample.

Similar sets of terms apply to the hiring of goods such as office equipment, cars, televisions, and videos.

5.2 SUPPLY OF GOODS AND SERVICES ACT 1982

If I contracted a builder to do some repair work in my house and he finished six months late, doubled the price contracted, and made a mess then he would have broken terms implied in the contract and I would not pay him more than a limited sum.

Doctor Proctor outlines... TERMS RELATING TO THE SALE OF SERVICES

Here we are concerned with contracts in which a person agrees to carry out a service. The most common complaints made in this area relate to the slowness with which the work is carried out, the cost of the work, and the poor quality of the work. Implied terms in contracts therefore relate to these areas.

Implied terms include:

1 A duty of care and skill, for example, that an estate agent or solicitor looks after the interests of their clients.

2 Reasonable time. That the service will be provided in a reasonable time limit.

3 Reasonable charges. That the charges for the service will be reasonable.

5.3 Sale and Supply of Goods to Consumers Regulations 2002

Key Ideas 🔑

Burden of proof

This is a new piece of consumer legislation which took effect from March 2003. The regulations implement the EU Directive of 1999 on the Sale of Consumer Goods and Associated Guarantees. UK law already covered much of the EU Directive because consumers already have an immediate right to reject goods and to demand their money back, when the goods are of unsatisfactory quality or not as described.

Doctor Proctor outlines... Main changes made in the Regulations

The main changes of the new Regulations are:

1. For the first six months after purchase/delivery, the burden of proof when reporting faulty goods is reversed in the consumer's favour. The regulations therefore insert a new rule into the Sale of Goods Act. This states that where goods sold to a consumer do not conform to the contract of sale 'at any time within the period of six months starting with the date on which the goods were delivered to the buyer', they must be taken not to have so conformed at that date. (Exclusions are 'that if it was established that they did not conform at that date', and 'its application is incompatible with the nature of the goods or the nature of the lack of conformity'.)

In addition, there is a right to have goods repaired or replaced or have a price reduction. These remedies are already widely used in the UK but they have not had status in law. Many suppliers in the interests of good customer relations allow customers to return goods. This right to reject unsatisfactory goods within a reasonable time is maintained. Where goods do not conform then the buyer may require the seller to repair or replace them. In many cases, repairs to cheap consumer goods are not worth doing and a replacement is the most sensible remedy for the seller.

These changes relate both to the Sale of Goods Act and to the Supply of Goods and Services Act.

2. Guarantees offered by manufacturers or retailers must be legally binding, written in plain language, and provide clear detail on how to claim (including the name and address of the guarantor). The guarantee must also be available on request.

Where goods are sold to a consumer with a consumer guarantee, the consumer guarantee takes effect at the time the goods are delivered 'as a contractual obligation owed by the guarantor under the conditions set out in the guarantee statement and the associated advertising'.

This EU Directive that has been built into UK law will protect UK shoppers abroad by providing a minimum standard of protection throughout the EU that was not available before.

5.4 CONSUMER PROTECTION ACT 1987

Key Ideas 🔑

Defective goods

This Act protects consumers against defective goods, including goods within the Sale of Goods Act, and a range of other goods such as crops and intangible goods such as electricity supply as well as components. The Act provides for liability for damage if goods do not meet the required standards and cause harm to people.

The Act bans the supply of unsafe goods and sets out that suppliers of goods that are found to be harmful must warn the public of the dangers.

The Consumer Protection Act is designed to encourage producers to supply safe goods which are free from defects and gives consumers the right to seek remedies when producers fail in this duty.

Doctor Proctor outlines... THE CASE THAT THE PLAINTIFF MUST PRESENT

The plaintiff must show that:

1 The product contained the stated defect.

2 The plaintiff suffered damage as a result.

3 The product caused the damage.

4 The defendant was the producer of the good.

The term **producer** refers to the manufacturer of the good but anyone who puts their trade mark on to goods which they purport to be the producer of is held to be the producer. However, if the person who puts their trade mark on an item with a label stating 'made for Super Supermarkets by Jones Producers' – then it will be Jones who will be liable.

A '**defect**' exists when a product's safety is not that 'which a reasonable person might be entitled to expect' and applies to the following:

1 Defects in design of the product.

2 Defects in the processing or manufacturing of the product.

3 Defects that are inherent in the product, where warning is not given.

The Act states that 'safety in relation to a product, shall include safety in respect to – components and safety in the context of risks of damage to property, as well as in the context of risks of death or personal injury.'

There are a number of defences that can be put forward by a producer defending a particular action, for example, that the defect was caused by a legal requirement, or that goods were not supplied for business purposes, such as scones made for a bring and buy charity stall.

In addition to the Consumer Protection Act, there are other pieces of legislation which apply specifically to given areas of safety, such as the Toy Safety Act, which for example, stops producers from using dangerous pins in children's toy teddy bears.

5.5 TRADE DESCRIPTIONS ACT 1968

The description given of the goods forms part of the contract between the buyer and the seller. This Act makes it a criminal offence for a trader to describe goods falsely. A type of case frequently prosecuted under this Act is the turning back of the 'clock' on a used car to disguise the mileage.

The two main offences covered by the Act are:

1   Applying false trade descriptions to goods or supplying goods with such a description.

2   Making false statements about the provision of services, accommodation or facilities.

It is important to note that this Act is concerned with criminal offences, rather than civil disputes between parties. The law applies only to suppliers in the course of a trade or business (not to private suppliers). However, the Act protects anyone who receives goods, whether they be an individual consumer or a business.

The Act states that a 'false description' is one that is 'false to a material degree'.

What this means is that if the description is misleading then it is likely to be regarded as being false to a material degree.

Doctor Proctor outlines... AREAS THAT THE ACT RELATES TO

The Act sets out that trade descriptions relate to the following aspects of descriptions of goods or parts of goods:

Description	Example
i) quantity and size	e.g. sizes of trainers
ii) method of making or processing	e.g. cooked in a tandoori oven
iii) composition i.e. what it is made of	e.g. a 100% cotton shirt
iv) fitness for purpose such as strength or performance	e.g. 16 megabyte hard drive
v) tests and results of tests that have been carried out	e.g. meets British Standards
vi) approval by a particular individual	e.g. as worn by Gary Lineker
vii) place or date of manufacture	e.g. 2004 VW Beetle
viii) person who produced the good	e.g. manufactured by Volkswagen
ix) other aspects of descriptions	

5.5 TRADE DESCRIPTIONS ACT 1968

In the case *Holloway* v. *Cross* (1981) the court ruled that a motor dealer who had bought a car with a mileage reading 716, and who estimated on an invoice that it had done 45,000 miles when it had really done 70,000, had given a false description.

The Trade Descriptions Act also includes advertising, under a section which relates to cases in which a trader 'uses the trade description in any manner likely to be taken as referring to the goods'.

The Act also covers the description of services which are provided in the course of a trade or business.

The Trading Standards Department or Consumer Protection Services Department of local authorities have power to investigate complaints about false or misleading descriptions or prices and other matters. Trading Standards Officers have a responsibility to enforce the Act and take offenders to court, which can lead to fines and imprisonment.

The description of a good should be seen as part of the contract.

5.6 WEIGHTS AND MEASURES ACT 1985

Key Ideas 🔑

Caveat emptor

This looks like a short measure to me!

The weight of an item is how much it weighs on the scales. Sometimes traded items will have a high weight such as that of a sack of potatoes. Other times the weighing process will require a highly sensitive scale because the weight is so small, such as the weight of a precious jewel, or a pharmaceutical substance. Measures relate to quantities given – e.g. measures of a liquid such as a litre of petrol.

Providing false weights and measures of goods has been around since trading began.

In the early days the principle of **'caveat emptor'** – 'let the buyer beware' – was the only rule that applied.

However, in the course of time, giving illegal weights and measures became a criminal offence.

The job of making sure that fair weights and measures are being given is the job of specialist Weights and Measures Inspectors who work closely with the Trading Standards Department.

Weights and Measures Inspectors will investigate complaints and systematically check traders who are selling items involving weights and measures. Examples of their work would be checking on pub optics, to check that the measures of whisky that are being provided match what the consumer expects. Offences might include putting too large a head on a pint of beer so that the consumer receives a short measure. Weights and Measures Inspectors would also check on petrol pumps to ensure that short measures are not being given.

Weights and Measures Inspectors also have the job of checking scales and other weighing devices in shops, market stalls and farms to check for their accuracy.

Pre-packed items must have a declaration of the quantity and weight contained within the pack. It is an offence to give short weight. Wrongly labelling packaging can be an offence both under the Trade Descriptions Act and the Weights and Measures Act.

5.7 CONSUMER CREDIT ACT 1974

Credit

We live in a society in which many people buy items on credit, ranging from their house and their car, to television sets, computers, and other electronic items as well as buying other shopping on credit cards.

Consumer Credit arrangements are defined by the Act as: 'credit agreements made between an individual (the 'debtor') and any other person (the 'creditor') by which the creditor provides the debtor with credit not exceeding £15,000'. The term individual does not include companies.

Example

Some common credit arrangements:

Bank loan: An individual borrows a sum of money for a period of time, e.g. two years, and then pays back so much a month which includes repayment of the sum borrowed + interest.

Overdraft: An individual takes out more than they have in their bank account up to an 'overdraft limit', e.g. £1,000. They are charged interest on the amount that they are overdrawn on a day-to-day basis, and will need to repay the overdraft.

Credit Card: e.g. Visa or Access. Borrower is given a credit limit. They can borrow up to this limit by using their card to make payments. At the end of the month they receive a statement. They are charged interest on the sum borrowed if it is not paid off immediately.

Store Card: A shopper can take out a store card and buy items in that shop on credit. They are then billed at the end of the month and will be charged interest on money not immediately repaid.

Hire-purchase: An individual arranges to hire an item such as a car. Usually they put down a deposit and borrow the remainder. They then repay the loan to a Finance Company over a period of time, paying interest on the loan. They don't own the item until the final repayment has been made.

Credit Sale: An individual buys an item on credit. They own the item straight away, e.g. an item of clothing. They then repay with interest over a period of time.

These credit arrangements are described by the Act as regulated agreements.

The Consumer Credit Act 1974 is designed to create a framework of rules governing these and other credit arrangements. The Act:

1 Regulates the formation, terms and enforcement of credit agreements.

2 Requires those giving credit to be licensed.

3 Sets out that advertisements for credit must show the true cost of the credit arrangement.

4 Sets out restrictions on doorstep selling, i.e. people selling to your door must be licensed.

5.7 CONSUMER CREDIT ACT 1974

To ensure that the debtor is fully aware of the agreement that they are getting involved with there are a number of legal requirements. These include:

- Information about:

    - the total charge for credit, e.g. £1,000 over two years.

    - the Annual Percentage Rate of Charge (APR), e.g. 20% APR.

    - the price at which goods could be bought for cash.

This information enables the borrower to compare the cash price with the credit price.

- Provision of a clear and detailed agreement setting out all the terms.

- The agreement can only be signed by the two parties when all the details in it have been filled in.

- The debtor must receive a written copy of the agreement.

Doctor Proctor outlines... HOW AN AGREEMENT CAN BE CANCELLED

The debtor:

In the past, salesmen were able to put a lot of pressure on people to sign up to what they thought were good deals, e.g. to buy a set of encyclopaedias for the children or double glazing at a good price. The next day or shortly after, the buyer might regret signing the deal.

Under the 1974 law the debtor is able to send a written notice cancelling the agreement within five days of receiving a copy of the agreement. The debtor is then entitled to a refund of their deposit, but must return the goods or arrange for them to be collected by the seller.

The creditor:

Creditors may wish to terminate an agreement if the debtor is failing to make payments.

Firstly the creditor must issue a default notice which sets out:

- how much is required to bring payments up to date;

- the time required to make payments;

- what will happen if the debt is not paid.

If the debtor pays up then they will not have broken the contract and it can continue.

However, if the debtor is still in breach, then the creditor may seek to recover possession of the goods, or to claim further sums of money from the debtor.

In the case of a hire-purchase agreement, if the debtor has already paid a third of the total price of the goods then the goods cannot be reclaimed and the creditor must seek financial compensation.

5.8 DATA PROTECTION ACT 1998

Key Ideas

Data Protection Principles

The **Data Protection Act** places obligation on those people and organisations who record and use personal data.

The Act applies only to the processing of data by computer, and only applies to personal data about living individuals. 'Personal data' includes expressions of opinion about an individual but not an indication of the intentions of the data user in respect of that individual.

These people are referred to in the Act as 'data users'. Data users must be open about their use of the data by telling the Data Protection Registrar (the person responsible for enforcing the Act) that they are collecting personal data and how they intend to use it.

Data users must register the following information with the registrar:

name and address

nature of data held, and purposes for which it is kept and used

sources from which the data was obtained

persons to whom the data has been disclosed

transfer of data overseas, and

one or more addresses for the receipt of requests from data subjects for access to data

The data user must abide by the data protection principles.

5.8 DATA PROTECTION ACT 1998

Doctor Proctor outlines... THE DATA PROTECTION PRINCIPLES

1 Information to be contained in personal data shall be obtained, and should be processed, fairly and lawfully.

2 Personal data should be held only for specified and lawful purposes.

3 Personal data which is held for any purpose/s should not be disclosed for any matter incompatible with that purpose/s.

4 Personal data held for a given purpose/s should be adequate, relevant and not excessive in relation to that purpose/s.

5 Personal data should be accurate, and where necessary, kept up to date.

6 Personal data shall not be kept for longer than required for the purpose/s that it is kept.

7 Individuals are entitled:

a) at reasonable intervals and without undue delay or expense:

i) to be informed by any data user whether he holds personal data to which that individual is the subject.

ii) to have access to any such data held by a data user, and

b) where appropriate to have such data corrected or erased.

8 There must be appropriate security measures to prevent unauthorised access to, or alteration, disclosure or destruction of, personal data and against accidental loss or destruction of personal data.

Doctor Proctor outlines... THE RIGHTS OF DATA SUBJECTS

A **data subject** is an individual who is the subject of personal data. They have a number of rights:

1 Access to personal data. They can apply to receive a copy of that data in intelligible form.

2 Compensation for inaccuracy. A data subject who suffers damage as a result of the inaccuracy of personal data is entitled to compensation from the data user for damage or distress.

3 Compensation for loss or unauthorised disclosure. The data subject can bring an action for compensation – for example, if they have been refused credit because a dater user has mistaken the details of Bryan Jones with those of Brian Jones, and as a result Bryan Jones was prevented from borrowing money.

5.9 ENVIRONMENT ACT 1995

Key Ideas 🔑

Duty of care

In 1987 the Single European Act made environmental policy a normal EU responsibility for the first time. EU regulations have increasingly impacted on the national legal frameworks for the environment in all Member States.

The Environment is increasingly creeping up the legislative agenda as we begin to realise the possible effects of ignoring environmental concerns.

In 1990, the UK's Environmental Protection Act set out to introduce major changes in this area, particularly in relation to pollution control and waste management. The Act created two new systems for regulating industrial pollution. Integrated Pollution Control (IPC) applied to more than 5,000 existing industrial processes with the largest pollution potential. It regulated all their releases to land, water and air and was enforced by an Inspectorate of Pollution. The second system was enforced by local authorities and covered 27,000 complex processes controlling emission to the air. Under both systems, operators had to employ the 'best available techniques not entailing excessive cost', to minimise releases of the most polluting substances, and to 'render harmless' all releases from their processes.

The 1995, the Environment Act continued this process of creating an integrated system for the control of pollution and waste by establishing the Environment Agency, bringing together the National Rivers Authority and Her Majesty's Inspectorate of Pollution.

Doctor Proctor outlines... SOME OF THE IMPACTS OF ENVIRONMENTAL LEGISLATION ON BUSINESS

European Union regulations have led to a flood of new laws in this country. In particular the Environment Protection and the Pollution Prevention and Control regulations have placed legal obligations on businesses and the processes that they carry out. For example, all companies involved in wood treatment need to have a permit which sets out strict controls on the releases from these processes and sets out conditions for monitoring and record keeping.

There are also strict controls on waste under a business' 'duty of care'. All industrial wastes must be identified, documented and only transported by carriers that are authorised to do so. There are

additional regulations for special wastes such as toxic materials. In addition, the Water Resources Act protects 'controlled waters' which include rivers, lakes, coastal seas and groundwater. It is an offence for businesses to discharge waste into these controlled waters without consent (which sets out the types, limits, and outlets into which waste can be discharged). There are also controls on what can be put down the sink and into drains. Businesses that fail to comply are faced with heavy fines and in the worst case prison sentences. Firms can also be prosecuted for failing to minimise the material that they use in the packaging of their products.

5.10 THE SMALL CLAIMS COURT AND THE COUNTY COURT

Key Ideas 🔑

Small claims

The county courts deal with less serious civil cases. These courts hear a large number of cases each year and are governed by the County Courts Act 1984.

Each county court is presided over by a circuit judge. Typically the judge will sit alone, although there is provision for trial by a jury of persons in some cases, for example, in cases of fraud. The judge is helped by a district judge who may try some cases and in others acts as a clerk of the court.

A large number of consumer related disputes are settled in the county courts, particularly those related to contract. Actions should be started in the county court in the geographical region where the defendant lives. Typical cases involving consumer issues would include claims with a value of not more than £5,000 (if all parties consent to what is known as a small claims track, larger sums can be dealt with).

You can use the small claims procedure if your claim is for £5,000 or less. This procedure is informal and can be conducted without solicitors, with hearings generally taking place in public. Expenses, but not legal costs such as solicitor's fees, are normally awarded to the successful side.

Where cases are more complex and involve bigger sums of money they will typically be heard in the High Court.

The small claims track is particularly suitable for taking less important cases to court.

One of the main purposes of county courts is to cut down the cost of taking a case to court. Many cases can be put forward by the parties themselves rather than employing legal council.

5.10 THE SMALL CLAIMS COURT AND THE COUNTY COURT

Small claims would involve:

- Straightforward cases that are easy to prepare.

- Claims with a relatively small value – less than £5,000.

- Cases where the costs are hoped to be kept low as the costs are not generally recoverable.

Typically lawyers and experts are not involved in small claims, although it is possible to get some advice, often for a fixed fee.

Generally only the fixed cost of issuing the claim is recoverable – although the court can ask for other costs to be recovered, e.g. costs of experts, travelling expenses, etc.

Small claims are usually heard by a district judge.

Dr Proctor says:
'You Must Know This!'

If you wish to pursue the small claims procedure you should fill in a claim form giving brief details of your claim, then take or send it to your local county court.

The necessary forms and leaflets are available from the Court Service website and court offices (look under 'courts' in the telephone books for addresses).

Your local Citizens Advice Bureau or consumer advice centre can give you help and advice with the forms. Some may also give free legal advice and offer someone to go to court with you.

The idea of the small claims track is to encourage people like you and me to take action when we feel we have been unfairly treated in consumer issues.

Unit 5.1: Sale of Goods Act 1979

1   What are the three main requirements relating to the selling of goods covered by the Sale of Goods Act?

2   If you took a suit to the dry cleaners and it was not ready two weeks later would you have cause for complaint?

3   If you take in a watch to be repaired and when you receive the repair bill it is for £200 do you have cause for complaint?

Unit 5.2: Supply of Goods and Services Act 1982

1   If a double glazing seller shows you a sample of work supplied by her company what rights should you expect if you agree to have windows installed by that company?

2   Explain two of the terms implied in a contract for the transfer of goods, work and materials.

Unit 5.3: The Sale and Supply of Goods to Consumers Regulations 2002

1   What are the two main changes brought in by these regulations?

2   How does this law protect UK citizens abroad?

Unit 5.4: Consumer Protection Act 1987

Which of the following statements about the Consumer Protection Act are true?

i)   The Act is designed to encourage producers to supply safe goods.

ii)   The plaintiff can make a case even if they haven't suffered damages.

iii) A defect might include a design defect.

iv)   A producer can defend themselves by showing that a defect is a result of a legal requirement.

v)   The Act provides for liability for damage if goods cause harm to people.

Unit 5.5: The Trade Descriptions Act 1968

1   What types of court would typically deal with offences under this Act?

2   List four aspects of descriptions that would be covered by this Act.

3   Which local authority body typically supervises this Act?

Unit 5.6: Weights and Measures Act 1985

1   What is meant by the principal of 'caveat emptor'?

2   Are issues involving false weights and measures simply a case of caveat emptor today?

3   What is meant by a measure?

Unit 5.7: Consumer Credit Act 1974

1   Give an example of a credit arrangement covered by this Act.

2   Can anybody give credit to consumers, e.g. by starting up a new credit card?

3   Give three examples of information that someone taking out credit would expect to receive.

4   What can someone who decides to sign an agreement to buy a car do to pull out of the agreement?

5   Could a finance company that had provided the finance for someone to buy a car repossess the car if the borrower has only paid back one tenth of the agreed sum and has fallen back on payments?

Unit 5.8: Data Protection Act 1998

1   Who are data users?

2   Give four examples of types of information that data users must register.

3   Explain one of the rights of a data subject.

Unit 5.9: Environment Act 1995

1   Which industrial processes is IPC principally targeted at?

2   What was the body that was created by bringing together the National Rivers Authority and Her Majesty's Inspectorate of Pollution?

3   Give three examples of controlled waters.

Unit 5.10: The Small Claims Court and the County Court

Which of the following statements are true?

i)   The county courts deal with the most serious civil cases.

ii) Cases tried in the county courts never involve a jury.

iii) A large number of consumer related cases are settled in the county courts.

iv) Cases involving very large sums of money are tried in the High Court.

v) The county courts aim to cut down the costs of going to court.

vi) A small claims procedure can be used for simple cases.

vii) Individuals can represent their own cases in small claims procedures.

viii) Usually only the fixed cost of issuing a claim is recoverable in a small claim.

ix) An individual would be unwise to pursue a case using small claims procedure because of the high cost involved.

You need to know the main Acts and how they affect the legal responsibilities of the business towards employment protection, dismissal, trade union membership rights and equal opportunities. There is a great deal of legislation in this area so we simply examine a few major exemplar pieces of legislation.

Topics covered in this unit

6.1 Sex Discrimination Acts 1975 and 1986

The Sex Discrimination Acts and the Race Relations Act share a number of common features, particularly in relation to the non-tolerance of discrimination in the workplace. The Sex Discrimination Act states that it is unlawful to treat someone less favourably on the basis of his or her sex.

6.2 Race Relations Act 1976

The Race Relations Act outlaws discrimination on the basis of racial grounds which the act defines as being on the basis of colour, race, nationality, or ethnic or national origin.

6.3 Equal Pay Act 1970

The Equal Pay Act, which has subsequently been amended by the Sex Discrimination Acts, requires equal treatment in terms of pay, holidays, sick pay and hours of work.

6.4 Employment Protection (Consolidation) Act 1978, updated by the Trade Union Reform and Employment Rights Act 1996

The Employment Rights Act is concerned to provide a range of protections for employees in the workplace, many of which relate to the contract of employment and resulting working conditions.

6.5 Disability Discrimination Act 1995

It is against the law for employers to discriminate against employees or prospective employees on account of disability.

6.6 Working Time Regulations and Directive 1993

In line with European Union requirements the Working Time Directive was introduced in 1999 which guaranteed all employees a maximum working week of 48 hours and also guaranteed everyone, including part-time workers, an annual four weeks' holiday.

6.1 SEX DISCRIMINATION ACTS 1975 AND 1986

Key Ideas

Discrimination

The Sex Discrimination Acts (SDAs) and the Race Relations Act (RRA) have a number of similarities and, because of this, they are often interpreted in the same way by employment tribunals. The RRA and SDAs both protect all employees irrespective of age or status, whether they are full- or part- time workers or have a fixed or temporary contract.

Sex discrimination

The Sex Discrimination Act states that it is unlawful to treat someone else less favourably on the basis of his or her sex:

'A person discriminates against a woman if, on the grounds of her sex, he treats her less favourably than he treats a man.' This applies equally to men and women.

In the twenty-first century both men and women are increasingly taking up issues of sex discrimination through tribunals.

Doctor Proctor outlines... THE NATURE OF DISCRIMINATION

The SDAs and the RRA attempt to deal with three sorts of discrimination:

1 Direct discrimination,

2 Indirect discrimination, and

3 Victimisation.

Direct discrimination occurs when one employee or candidate for a job is treated better or more favourably than another because of his or her race or sex. For example, a British Asian applies for a job as a carpenter and he goes for an interview at a building site. He is told there they 'don't employ blacks' and he wouldn't fit in. This is a prime example of race discrimination.

Indirect discrimination takes place when all employees seem to be treated exactly the same on the surface but, when looked at closer, members of a particular racial group or gender are found to be discriminated against. This might occur when an employer applies conditions or requirements to a job which clearly discriminate against certain groups. For example, an employer tries to insist that all female staff may not wear trousers at work. Clearly, this will disadvantage groups whose culture or religion requires that legs should be covered up.

Victimisation occurs when an employee is singled out for unfair treatment because he or she has attempted to exercise rights under the RRA, SDA or Equal Pay Act, or has helped others to enforce their rights. For example, if an employee were to appear as a witness or to support another employee's claim for discrimination and as a result was not chosen for promotion within an organisation.

6.1 SEX DISCRIMINATION ACTS 1975 AND 1986

Exceptions to the Sex Discrimination Act

The main exceptions where discrimination is permitted are as follows:

- Jobs that for genuine reasons must be carried out by someone of a particular sex.

- Privacy or decency is required (e.g. a changing-room attendant).

- Single-sex hospitals, prisons or care centres.

- Jobs that involve work in a country whose laws require individuals to be of a certain sex.

Sex discrimination also relates to job advertising and you may sometimes see the following insert in a national newspaper:

SEX DISCRIMINATION ACTS

No job advertisement which indicates or can reasonably be understood as indicating an intention to discriminate on ground of sex (e.g. by inviting applicants only from males or only from females) may be accepted, unless it is exempted from the requirements of the Sex Discrimination Act.

A statement must be made at the time the advertisement is placed saying which of the exceptions in the Act is considered to apply. It is the responsibility of the advertisers to ensure that advertisement content does not discriminate under the terms of the Sex Discrimination Acts.

Enforcement

Individuals or groups who feel that they have been discriminated against can complain to an employment tribunal within three months of the date of the act that they are complaining about. Initially a conciliation officer will try to resolve the dispute without having a tribunal hearing. It is also now possible for the employer and employee to reach a compromise contract which is a binding agreement whereby the employee waives the right to continue with the claim.

An employment tribunal may make an order declaring the rights of the parties in dispute in relation to the complaint. The tribunal can also make an order for compensation without limits, to cover such things as loss of prospective earnings and injured feelings.

The Equal Opportunities Commission was set up to promote equal opportunities and to make sure that the Sex Discrimination Act and the Equal Pay Act are given teeth. The Commission has powers to hold formal investigations, and, when it finds cases which are unlawful, to issue non-discrimination notices setting out that they must cease. The Commission has powers to require people to attend and to give evidence.

6.2 RACE RELATIONS ACT 1976

Key Ideas

Genuine Occupational Qualifications

The Race Relations Act (RRA) states that:

'A person discriminates against another if, on racial grounds, he treats another less favourably than he treats, or would treat another person.'

Discrimination on racial grounds is, for the purpose of the RRA, defined as discrimination on the basis of colour, race, nationality, or ethnic or national origin.

Racial discrimination includes 'inducement to discriminate' as highlighted by the following case:

Exceptions to the Race Relations Act

The Act recognises that, for certain jobs, being a member of a particular racial group can be a necessary requirement for the particular job. These exceptions are known as Genuine Occupational Qualifications (GOQs) – for example, being an Italian to work in an Italian restaurant. GOQs relate to entertainers, actors, actresses, artists' and photographers' models, waiters and waitresses.

Enforcement

Individuals who have been the subject of unlawful conduct can take their complaint to an employment tribunal. Complaints about the provision of goods, facilities and services can be made to the county court.

In addition, the Commission for Racial Equality (CRE), which works to eliminate discrimination and promote equality of opportunity and good race relations, can take various actions, including:

- issuing of non-discrimination notices

- taking cases to employment tribunals and to the county courts

- seeking injunctions in the county court against persistent discrimination.

The Public Order Act of 1986 makes it a criminal offence to stir up racial hatred anywhere by use of words or behaviour or display of written material. This would include graffiti in the workplace.

The Commission for Racial Equality v. Imperial Society of Teachers of Dancing (1983)

In this case the Imperial Society wanted to employ a filing clerk. They rang the local girls' school to find a 'suitable applicant'. During the call the representative of the Imperial Society made it clear that a 'coloured girl' would not fit in because they did not employ any 'coloured employees'. The Employment Tribunal held that the words 'to induce' in the Race Relations Act applied in this case in that the Imperial Society were seeking 'to induce' the careers teacher at the school not to send a 'coloured girl'. The Imperial Society were thus held to have contravened the RRA.

6.3 EQUAL PAY ACT 1970

Key Ideas 🔑

Equal pay categories

The objective of the EPA was fundamentally to ensure that women receive the same pay as men for the same or broadly similar work. If a woman (or man) wants to make a claim for pay discrimination, she must ensure that whatever man she compares herself to is in the same employment (i.e. the man has to be employed by the same employer or an associated employer).

The EPA establishes that contracts of employment are regarded to contain an equality clause operating on pay when women are employed on 'like work' or work 'rated as equivalent' (which can be evaluated by a job evaluation study).

The 1983 EPA Amendment regulations added a further case where women are employed in work which in terms of the demands of the job (e.g. skill, effort, and decision making) is of equal value to that done by a man in the same employment.

Where an equal pay claim is successful in an Employment Tribunal then the complainant has a contractual right to the higher pay and other terms. However, back pay can only be claimed for up to two years from the date of application to the Tribunal.

In recent years the concept of equal pay has also been applied to pensions, based on an Article in the Treaty of Rome. One effect of this ruling has been to lead many companies to increase the pensionable age for women to 65 to create equality with men.

In recent times we have also seen an extension of equality of treatment to include part-time workers under the Part-time Employees (Prevention of Less Favourable Treatment) Regulations 2000. The resulting rights of part-time employees under these regulations include:

- The right to receive the same hourly rate of pay as comparable full-time workers.

- The same hourly rate of overtime pay.

- The same rights to sick pay and maternity pay.

- Equal access to pension rights and pension schemes.

- Equal access to training.

- Pro-rata entitlements to leave, holidays and breaks.

- Part-time employees should not be treated less favourably in relation to redundancy.

Doctor Proctor outlines... EQUAL PAY ACT CATEGORIES

The purpose of the EPA is to make sure that women are given the same treatment as men:

- Who are engaged in like work in the same employment.

- Whose work is rated as equivalent.

- Whose work is otherwise of equal value.

Pay is defined under the EPA as including:

- fringe benefits or the use of a car

- sick pay

- redundancies or severance pay

- the right to join a pension scheme.

6.4 Employment Rights Act 1996

The Employment Rights Act, subsequently amended by the Employment Relations Acts of 1999 and 2003, provides a range of statutory rights for employees, which are of a contractual nature.

Pay

Employees are entitled to an itemised pay statement which sets out the gross pay, and deductions, and the net pay.

Example

		Weekly
Gross wage	=	£200
Tax + national insurance	=	£30
Pension contributions	=	£30
Net pay	=	£140

Employees are entitled to receive as a minimum, the National Minimum Wage which was established by the National Minimum Wage Act 1998, and is regularly increased in line with the cost of living.

Doctor Proctor outlines... THE MAIN FEATURES OF A CONTRACT OF EMPLOYMENT

The Employment Rights Act 1996 dictates that the terms and conditions that must be set out in writing are:

- The names of the employer and the employee.

- The date when the employment began.

- The scale or rate of pay and the method of calculating pay where the employee is paid by commission or bonus.

- When payment is made (i.e. weekly or monthly), and the day or date of payment.

- The hours to be worked, including any compulsory overtime.

- Holiday entitlement and holiday pay.

- Sick pay and injury arrangements.

- Entitlements to a pension scheme.

- The length of notice of termination an employee must receive or give.

- The job title.

- The duration of temporary contracts.

- The work location or locations.

- Grievance procedures.

- Disciplinary procedures.

An employee who does not receive written particulars can take the issue to an employment tribunal. The tribunal can make a declaration setting out what particulars must be provided.

6.4 EMPLOYMENT RIGHTS ACT 1996

Dismissal

Over the years, the rules for dismissing employees have become more and more complicated. The heart of the matter lies in the difference between what the courts regard to be 'fair' and 'unfair' dismissal.

Doctor Proctor outlines... 'FAIR DISMISSAL'

Fair dismissal can take place when an employee can be shown to be guilty of :

- Wilful destruction of company property
- Sexual or racial harassment
- Continuous bad timekeeping
- A negative attitude at work
- Inability to do the job
- Sleeping on the job.

In addition, an individual can be fairly dismissed for lack of capability or qualifications to do a particular job. This would typically come to light in the early stages of work where the employee shows lack of confidence. In some cases it might be shown that the employee has made false assertions about the qualifications that they hold.

In some cases (e.g. for bad timekeeping) employees would normally receive oral warnings, written warnings and even suspensions before dismissal.

Doctor Proctor outlines... 'UNFAIR DISMISSAL'

Unfair dismissal would almost certainly be deemed to have occurred in any of the following circumstances:

- Pregnancy: An employee can be sacked only if she is unable to do her job properly as a result of being pregnant.

- Race: A worker cannot be sacked on grounds of race.

- Homosexuality: A person should not be sacked on grounds of their sexual orientation.

- Union membership: An employer cannot sack a worker for belonging to a trade union. Neither can an employee be sacked for not belonging to a union or particular union.

- Criminal record: If an employer does not find out about an employee's criminal record until some time after employment starts, they cannot sack them unless they were convicted of a 'relevant' crime (e.g. a cashier who has a record of stealing petty cash).

- Asserting rights under the National Minimum Wage Act.

The Sunday Trading Act 1995 also stated that an employee could not be dismissed or made redundant for refusing to work on a Sunday.

For an employer to escape liability for unfair dismissal, they must show that they acted reasonably. The Employment Rights Act requires the employer to state the reasons for dismissal in writing.

6.4 EMPLOYMENT RIGHTS ACT 1996

The Trade Union and Labour Reform Act 1973

Many employees belong to trade unions. Individuals should be protected against unfair treatment for being a member of a union. At the same time, union members should not treat others unfairly.

The Trades Union and Labour Reform Act and the Employment Rights Act attempted to support consumers' rights and protect business from union action with the following measures:

- The right for workers to have a postal ballot on union action and the right not to have union subscriptions deducted without consent.

- The right for workers not to be expelled or excluded from a union other than for certain reasons, such as not belonging to a certain trade as stated in union rules.

- The right for employers to have seven days' notice of industrial action.

- The right for people deprived of goods or services by industrial action to take action to prevent it happening.

Under the Employment Relations Act 1999, employers have to recognise trade unions where at least 40 per cent of those eligible to do so take part in a ballot, and a majority of those voting are in favour of recognition. In organisations where already more than 50 per cent of the workforce were union members there was automatic recognition.

The Employment Relations Act gives protection against dismissal for individuals campaigning on behalf of their unions – and unions are allowed reasonable access to employees.

Employers can make an agreement with a recognised union to deduct members' subscriptions to the union directly from pay, providing the relevant workers have given written approval.

Health and Safety at Work

All employees are entitled to work in healthy and safe working conditions.

The Health and Safety at Work Act 1974 is the most important law governing issues related to health and safety. This Act is supervised by the Health and Safety Commission. More recently, Health and Safety requirements have been updated by a series of European Union Directives.

Most importantly, Health and Safety regulations were set out in 1992 in a series of measures known as the 'six pack'. These regulations set out the general duties that employers have to their employees and members of the public, as well as obligations that employees have to each other.

The Management of Health and Safety Regulations 1997 set out clearly what managers have to do in relation to every work activity.

6.4 EMPLOYMENT RIGHTS ACT 1996

Doctor Proctor outlines... RISK ASSESSMENT

The main requirements of Health and Safety regulations in this country are that:

- Every employer with five or more employees must carry out a 'risk assessment'.

- The employer must then take health and safety measures in line with the risk assessment.

- The employer must appoint competent people to help carry out the health and safety arrangements.

- Employers must set up emergency procedures.

- Employers must provide clear information and training to employees.

- Employers must work jointly with other employers sharing the same premises.

A written safety policy

In law, if an organisation employs five or more people, it must have a written safety policy. This must set out:

- Who is responsible for workplace health and safety.

- The arrangements that have been made for health and safety.

This policy must also be communicated to everyone in the workplace. Employees also have a responsibility for safety. They must comply with company arrangements and procedures for securing a safe workplace. They must report to management incidents that have led, or may lead, to injury. And, they must co-operate in the investigation of accidents in order to prevent them happening again.

6.5 DISABILITY DISCRIMINATION ACT 1995

Key Ideas

Disabled person

Over the years, legislation governing the disabled has been widely ignored by employees. For example, employers have often sought to get round disability legislation requiring quotas for employment by providing disabled people with 'suitable work' such as lift and car park attendants. By the 1990s, disability increasingly came to be seen as an equal opportunities issue.

Section 1 of the Act defines a disabled person as 'a person who has a physical or mental impairment which has a substantial and long-term effect on his or her ability to carry out normal day-to-day activities. It also states that the impairment is of long-term effect if it has lasted for 12 months or is likely so to last or is likely to last for life.

The 1995 Disability Discrimination Act makes it unlawful to discriminate on grounds of disability in employment. The law requires employers of more than 20 people to accommodate the needs of the disabled and it established a right of access for the disabled in transport, higher education and some other areas.

The law also created a National Disability Council to provide advice on freeing the disabled from discrimination.

The Act defines discrimination in relation to disability as when a disabled person is treated less favourably by the discriminator than he or she treats or would treat others (and he or she cannot show that the treatment is justified).

The Act relates to the holding of company meetings by public companies that may be expected to produce accounts in Braille and to provide access ramps to meetings for people in wheelchairs.

Enforcement of the Act is through the county courts.

Doctor Proctor outlines... HOW THE LAW APPLIES TO THE PROVISION OF GOODS, FACILITIES OR SERVICES

It is unlawful to discriminate against the disabled on account of their disability in the provision of goods, facilities or services.

Providers must take reasonable steps to:

- Change practices, policies or procedures which make it difficult or impossible for disabled people to use a service, e.g. travelling by bus.

- Remove any physical barriers that make it unreasonably difficult for disabled people to use a service.

- Provide other aids or services which make a service more accessible to the disabled.

A code of practice has been set out to help providers of goods, facilities and services to comply.

6.6 WORKING TIME REGULATIONS AND DIRECTIVE 1993

Key Ideas

Maximum hours

A worker is defined as a person working under a contract of service, but under the Regulations the majority of agency workers, and trainees engaged on work experience are covered.

The Working Time Regulations are part of the European Union's social policy to guarantee minimum working standards and thus to improve the quality of life for working people.

The Regulations define working time as 'time when a worker is working at his employer's disposal and carrying out his duty or activities.' Lunch breaks spent at leisure are not included but working breakfasts and lunches are. Time spent travelling to work is not likely to be considered as working time.

Doctor Proctor outlines... KEY ASPECTS OF THE REGULATIONS

The Working Time Regulations 1998 and the Young Workers Directive 1998 provide protection for employees with regard to the hours they can work.

These Working Time Regulations now provide that a person's average weekly working time (including overtime) should not have to exceed 48 hours, averaged over a period of 17 weeks. Individuals can agree to be excluded from the maximum working week requirements on a voluntary basis.

Night working should not have to exceed eight hours in each 24-hour period, over 17 weeks.

Adult workers must be permitted to take a rest period of not less than 11 consecutive hours in each 24-hour period, and a weekly rest period of not less than 24 hours in each seven-day period. Young workers are entitled to a daily rest period of 12 consecutive hours, except in unexpected and unpredictable occurrences where compensatory rest may be permitted within three weeks.

Doctor Proctor outlines... LEAVE ARRANGEMENTS

Maternity and paternity leave has been covered by recent European Union regulations. Employees must have completed one year's service before being entitled to parental leave. They are entitled to 13 weeks' parental leave to care for each child born or adopted after 15 December 1999. This regulation applies to mothers and fathers equally.

Leave can be taken at any time until the child's fifth birthday, or five years after the adoption date. Parents of disabled children can take leave until the child's eighteenth birthday.

Individuals taking maternity or paternity leave are guaranteed the right to return to the same job or similar with the same level or greater pay and benefits.

Unit 6.1: Sex Discrimination Acts 1975 and 86

1 State whether the following would involve a) Direct sex discrimination, b) Indirect sex discrimination, c) No discrimination

   i) An advert asking for friendly bar staff.

   ii) An advert for 'male applicants only'.

   iii) An advert stating that heavy lifting is required.

   iv) An advert stating applicants will not be considered who may want to take extended periods of leave.

   v) An advert for a male lead to play Hamlet in a play.

2 If an individual feels that sex discrimination has been applied against them what remedies do they have?

Unit 6.2: Race Relations Act 1976

1 Which of the following would be acceptable in law?

   i) An advertisement for a male secretary to work in Saudi Arabia.

   ii) An advertisement for a job in a local café – 'no ethnic minorities considered'.

   iii) An advertisment for a waiter in a Spanish restaurant – 'person of Spanish extraction required for waiting job'.

2 What is meant by a Genuine Occupational Qualification (GOQ)?

Unit 6.3: Equal Pay Act 1970

1 Give three items that would be considered under the heading 'pay' for the Equal Pay Act.

2 If a woman was doing a similar job to a man, and that work was rated by a job evaluation scheme as being of equal worth, would she be entitled by law to equal pay?

Unit 6.4: Employment Rights Act 1996

1 Identify six major features that are expected to appear in a contract of employment.

2 What rights does an employee have in relation to being informed about pay?

3 Give three reasonable causes of 'fair dismissal'.

4 How many days' notice are employees expected to give before taking industrial action?

5 What are the legal requirements for employer recognition of trade unions?

6 What is a risk assessment?

Unit 6.5: Disability Discrimination Act 1995

1 What responsibility do employers of more than 20 people have?

2 How does the Act define discrimination?

Unit 6.6: Working Time Regulations 1998

1 What is meant by 'working time'?

2 What is the maximum number of hours that an employee should be expected to work each week?

3 Can employees agree to work longer hours?

4 How long is statutory parental leave?

Answers

Unit 1 Introduction

The main sources of law that affect business

1 Legislation is made by the European Union's directives and regulations, and by Acts of Parliament, and bye-laws.
   Case law is made by judges.
2 The principle of equity is important as a form of protection.

Legislation by Act of Parliament

1 **a** Sometimes a Private Member but more usually the government of the day.
   b A committee of MPs.
   c The Queen.
2 Committees of MPs and the House of Lords.
3 A local council.
4 It means beyond the powers given to a particular body.

Cases decided in the courts

1 The European Court of Justice.
2 The House of Lords.
3 A magistrates' court.
4 So that other judges can understand the principles and build them into future case law.
5 Because they are not happy with the decision made lower down, and they believe that the higher court has more expertise in dealing with more complicated matters.

European Union treaties, directives and regulations

1 Primary legislation is made up of Treaties and other major agreements. Secondary legislation is the variety of procedures such as regulations and directives.
2 New legislation is primarily proposed by the Commission but, increasingly, the European Parliament is gaining powers to suggest new areas to the Commission.
3.

	Directly binding	Not binding	Binding to whom?
Regulations	■		Member States
Directives	■		Member States
Decisions	■		Relevant parties, e.g. Member States, businesses, etc.
Recommendations		■	

4 To strengthen the protection of individuals within the Union and to make sure that community laws are interpreted uniformly.

Criminal and civil courts

1 **a)** Criminal **b)** Civil (could be criminal if breach of Trade Descriptions) **c)** Civil **d)** Criminal **e)** Civil **f)** Criminal **g)** Civil

Unit 2 The Legal Status of Business Organisations

Sole traders

a The owner has unlimited liability. Tax returns must be made to the Inland Revenue which can be time consuming.
b An individual may use the sole trader form because it is easier to set up with fewer legal formalities and paperwork. They are their own boss and do not have to rely on others. They can make decisions on their own and all the profits are theirs.

Partnerships

1 An ordinary partnership would typically have – **c**, **e**, **g** and **h**.
2 A Deed of Partnership is usually drawn out, with the help of a solicitor.
3 If a partner dies in an ordinary partnership then the partnership will need to be reconstituted with a new Deed.

Franchises

1 The franchisor and the franchisee.
2 Someone taking out a franchise could trade under a well known name, receive materials, equipment and training from the franchisor. They would benefit from national promotion and advertising carried out on their behalf by the franchisor.
3 Coca-Cola can franchise out bottling operations while retaining strict quality controls on the franchisee. Coca-Cola are not tying up their own capital, and can concentrate on other activities such as marketing and promoting the brand.

Private and public companies

1 The shareholders are the owners.
2 A board of directors.
3 The executive directors are involved in decision making on a day-to-day basis, whereas non-executives simply bring their expertise and influence to board meetings when overall strategy may be decided.

4   Shareholders appoint directors but the MD plays a key role in selecting executive directors.

5   Limited liability gives ordinary shareholders the security of knowing that their personal wealth is not at risk – simply their share capital in the business.

6   Shareholders may want to replace a Board that has made unsound decisions, which has acted beyond its powers, and which has overseen the creation of poor results, a poor shareholder dividend and falling share price.

7   The following are not features of a company – **b**, and **f**.

Charities

1   WWF, Oxfam, War Child and Save the Children are some examples.

2   A Charity is a not-for-profit organisation that seeks to serve the wider community. Its objectivess do not include making a profit.

3   The following are features of charities – **b**, **c**, **f**, and **g**.

Unit 3 Laws Governing the Formation and Running of Businesses

Memorandum and Articles of Association

1   The promoters are the people wishing to set up a company. They do this through a solicitor in the form of (i) a tailor made, or (ii) off-the-peg company.

2   Items in the memorandum would include: name, registered office, objects of the company, liability of members and authorised share capital. Businesses dealing with the company, such as creditors and suppliers, might want to look at the memorandum.

3   Ultra vires means beyond the powers. This might be the case when the directors of a company went beyond what they were allowed to do by their memorandum and articles.

4   The articles show the internal workings of the company and are for company members and prospective shareholders.

Statutory books

1   The statutory books are the records of a company and include – a register of members, a register of directors, copies of the memorandum and articles and a register of the interests of directors.

2   The books are open to inspection by members, creditors and the general public.

Statutory contracts

1   A contract is a legal agreement between two or more parties, who promise to give and receive something from each other.

2   A statutory contract is the contract which a company makes by means of its memorandum and articles of association.

3   The articles provide a contract between the company and its members.

Partnership agreements

1   A partnership is a relationship between a group of people who are pursuing a common business interest to make a profit.

2   Limited liability partnerships are a new form of partnership which is a body corporate being distinguishable from its members.

3   It shares a number of features with a company – for example, it does not dissolve with the departure of a partner, and it has corporate status. The Limited Liability Partnership is registered with the Registrar of Companies. Members have limited liability.

The Companies Acts 1985 and 1989

1   Having corporate status means that the company is recognised in law as a body in its own right.

2   *Saloman* v. *Saloman and Co. Ltd* established the principle of the company as a body in its own right.

3   In a company limited by shares the members can only lose up to the value of their shareholding should it be liquidated. In a company limited by guarantee the liability is set out by a clause in the memorandum should the company be wound up.

4   The members are the shareholders who are listed on the shareholders register. Details include their names, addresses, the number of shares they hold and when they bought the shares.

5   Shareholders' rights include the ability to sell their shares, to receive notice of meetings, to receive dividends when appropriate, and to receive a copy of the annual report.

6   The Annual General Meeting, and an Extraordinary General Meeting.

7   An ordinary resolution requires a majority of over 50% of shareholders.

8   A special resolution may be brought in to change the articles of a company.

9   Company accounts must be kept and maintained at the company office. The annual report must include a balance sheet and profit and loss account that comply with the Companies Act, and are approved by the Board of Directors.

10 An administrator has powers to manage a company with the purpose of handing it over to new owners. A receiver is someone appointed to take over some of the company's assets in order to sell them off to meet the requirements of debtors who have requested the court to bring in a receiver to protect their interests.

11 Keeping a business as a going concern means that it continues to trade and do business rather than being forced to close down. Businesses that are kept as going concerns are much more attractive to potential buyers because the goodwill and momentum still resides in the company.

The Partnership Act 1890

1 The partners are liable for the debts as set out in the Deed of Partnership.
2 The partnership owns the property brought into it.
3 The Partnership Act sets out that the profits will be shared equally.
4 The consent of all partners is required for a new partner to join.
5 Disputes can be settled by the majority of partners.
6 Dormant partners may be retired members of the partnership. Salaried partners are really employees of the firm.

The Business Names Act 1985

1 Basic requirements include the ending Ltd or PLC, that names should not be the 'same' as those already registered or too similar. There are restrictions on the use of names such as 'Bank' which requires a special licence. Rude and offensive names aren't allowed.
2 Companies can change their name by special resolution.
3 An unacceptable name would be one that is offensive, or directly copies that of another company.
4 The courts frown on opportunistic use of names which involves taking away the goodwill of an existing company.
5 Names freely available for partnerships usually involve the names of the partners.

Legal responsibilities of key personnel in a business

1 A first director is someone who is in post when the company is set up.
2 New directors are appointed by a majority vote at an AGM.
3 Fiduciary responsibility is that of acting as a trustee in the best interests of a company.
4 The main duty of a director is to act responsibly in the best interests of their company.
5 Information disclosed about company directors includes – their names, addresses, occupations, number of shares in a company, and shareholding in other companies, as well as details of their service contract.
6 The Chair or Board of Directors will appoint the Managing Director.
7 The Company Secretary keeps company records, sends out notices about meetings and keeps the share register.

Unit 4 Contract Law

Standard forms of contract

1 A simple contract can be made by word of mouth or in writing.
2 An agreement exists when one party accepts another's offer.
3 Genuineness of consent involves freely entering into a contract rather than a forced relationship.
4 Because if a contract is void then it is not a contract.
5 An unenforceable contract is one that is valid but can't be enforced because one of the parties won't do what is required.
6 Contracts can be made for the supply of goods, the supply of work and materials, the supply of goods on credit or for the purpose of bailment.

Forming an agreement

1 Because the court recognised that an offer had been made to the whole world including Mrs Carlill and that it was a real offer.
2 An invitation to treat is when a company opens itself up to offers but is not bound to accept a particular offer.
3 Acceptance involves taking up an offer. Acceptance must be communicated to the offeror and be absolute and unqualified.
4 a) Jones cannot accept an offer made to someone else – acceptance can only be made for an offer made directly to an individual.
   b) I might not be able to accept an offer by sending an e-mail because the offer asks for another form of acceptance.

Capacity to contract and intention to create legal relations

1 Minors can enter into contracts for certain purposes, e.g. to buy goods from a shop. However, they cannot enter into contracts which are illegal, e.g. to buy a bottle of spirits from an off licence when they are under age.
2 A shopkeeper should not sell items to minors when these go beyond the minors' actual requirements.
3 Commercial agreements are generally binding, social and domestic agreements generally are not.

Consideration

1 If I give you £5 it will involve consideration if you agree to do something in return, e.g. give me a book.
2 Chocolate wrappers were considered adequate because this is what was offered when the bargain was struck.
3 No – because it is part of the teacher's duty to mark students' work – and he is already being paid to do this. If it was additional private work this would be different.

Illegality

1 A contract would be illegal if it involved a criminal offence. Additionally it would be illegal if it involved corruption, or trading with an enemy of the country.

2 Contracts preventing someone from working once a contract is completed. A sales agreement whereby the trader agrees to buy from only one seller.

3 Mistakes generally do not make contracts unavoidable.

4 A mistake might be a person thinking they have bought 10 tons of fertiliser when the other party believed they were selling 100 tons.

5 A puff is a form of sales hype – where a seller makes claims about how good their product is. A puff is generally not considered to be misrepresentation.

Duress and undue influence

1 Duress refers to violence or threat of violence.

2 Economic duress is where one party uses its power and size to put undue pressure on the other party.

3 Undue influence involves making a contract which one party does not enter into freely.

Exclusion clauses

1 If an exclusion clause is ambiguous the court will generally ignore the interpretation of the party that drew up the clause, favouring the other party's interpretation.

2 They will need to show that the other party agreed to it at the time the contract was made out.

3 The 'repugnancy rule' sets out that if a clause goes against the purposes of the contract then it should be struck out.

Express and implied terms

1 An implied term is one that is not expressly written into a contract but is part of customary behaviour or statute, or which the court believes was implied when the contract was made out.

2 The express terms would appear in writing or in quotable verbal statements.

3 Conditions are fundamental obligations in a contract whereas warranties are less important obligations. The conditions lie at the heart of the contract.

Termination of contract

1 Termination by agreement involves parties establishing from the outset when the contract would be terminated. Termination by performance involves establishing performance criteria that need to be met for completion of the contract.

2 Complete performance involves doing absolutely everything stipulated in the contract.

3 Frustration is when it is impossible to complete a contract.

4 Breach occurs when one party fails to perform their part of the agreement.

Arbitration

1 Arbitration may be cheaper and more importantly is done in private so that there is less adverse publicity associated with a dispute.

2 Arbitration can be costly because legal experts may be involved whose fees are high on a day-to-day basis.

Remedies

1 Damages are the compensation that must be provided to remedy the hurt to an injured party – they may be financial or involve some other form of compensation.

2 **a)** Liquidated damages are ones that are decided from the outset. **b)** Penalties are not necessarily related to the size of the damage but seek to penalise for poor performance in meeting contractual terms.

3 An injunction is a means of preventing someone from breaking a contract, often stopping them from carrying out an action that goes against the requirements of the contract.

The Misrepresentation Act

1 The Misrepresentation Act gave courts general powers to award damages in cases of non-fraudulent misrepresentation.

2 If misrepresentation is set out in the terms of a contract then an innocent party will have remedies through the courts for this misrepresentation. For example, if they have suffered a loss and if the person making the misrepresentation would normally be liable to damages then damages can be claimed.

The Unfair Contract Terms Act 1977

1 Factors considered in determining whether a contract is reasonable include the ability to make payment, and the relative strengths of the parties involved in the contract, and whether the contract is similar to those involved in previous dealings and customs of the trade.

2 Inducement to agree to the clause, and buyer's knowledge of the extent of the clause.

The Unfair Terms in Consumer Contracts Regulations 1994

1 Unfair terms are ones which cause a significant imbalance in the rights and obligations of the parties under the contract.

2 'The seller is not obliged to meet any of the terms set out in the contract'.

3 An unfair term is not binding on a consumer. However, the remainder of the contract may be if it is reasonable.

Unit 5 Consumer Protection Legislation

Sale of Goods Act 1979

1 The three main requirements are that goods should be:
- of satisfactory quality
- fit for the purpose, and
- as described.

2 Typically two weeks would be a long time to wait (unless the dry cleaners had told you that delays would be likely). Therefore it may be seen as not being ready in a 'reasonable time'.

3 A watch repair costing £200 would most likely be seen as an unreasonable charge.

Supply of Goods and Services Act 1982

1 You would expect the windows installed in your house to be the same or similar in quality to those shown in the sample.

2 The goods should be as described, and they should be fit for the purpose they are provided for. For example, a new central heating boiler should be of sufficient size and capacity to warm the house that it is being installed in.

Sale and Supply of Goods to Consumers Regulations 2002

1 The main changes brought by these regulations are that for the first six months after purchase or delivery the burden of proof when reporting faulty goods is in the consumer's favour, and that guarantees must be legally binding and written in plain English.

2 UK shoppers abroad are given the same minimum standard of protection that they would receive at home.

Consumer Protection Act 1987

The statements that are true are – **i**, **iii**, **iv** and **v**.

Trade Descriptions Act 1968

1 Offences are typically dealt with in a criminal court.

2 Four aspects covered are quantity and size, composition, fitness for purpose, and approval by a particular individual, e.g. David Beckham.

3 The Act is supervised by the Trading Standards Department.

Weights and Measures Act 1985

1 This means let the buyer beware or look out for themselves.

2 Today weights and measures are checked by weights and measures inspectors working for the local authority who can make prosecutions for the criminal offence of giving false weights and measures.

3 A measure would be something like a litre of petrol, or a given quantity of a spirit.

Consumer Credit Act 1974

1 An example of a credit agreement covered by the Act would be hire-purchase, or credit sale.

2 Providers of credit need to have a licence.

3 The total charge for credit, the APR and the cash price.

4 They can pull out of the agreement within five days which is regarded to be a cooling off period.

5 They can repossess the item for non-payment up to the time when a third has been paid. However, initially they would have to ask for payments to be kept up, giving the buyer the chance to abide by their side of the contract.

Data Protection Act 1998

1 People who record and use data are referred to as data users e.g. credit card companies, employers, etc.

2 Nature of data held, sources of data, person to whom the data has been disclosed, transfer of data overseas.

3 A data subject can apply to receive a copy of the data about them in an intelligible form.

Environment Act 1995

1 IPC is targeted at those industrial processes with the largest pollution potential.

2 The Environment Agency.

3 Rivers, groundwater and coastal seas.

The Small Claims Court and the County Court

The following statements are true – **iii**, **iv**, **v**, **vi**, **vii**, **viii**.

Unit 6 Employment Law

Sex Discrimination Acts 1975 and 1986

1 **i)** No discrimination.
 ii) Direct discrimination.
 iii) No discrimination.
 iv) Indirect discrimination.
 v) No discrimination.

2 They can take their case to an Employment Tribunal. A conciliation officer will seek to resolve the issue. The Tribunal can make an order for compensation without limits to cover loss of earnings and injured feelings.

Race Relations Act 1976

1   The following would be acceptable in law – **i** and **iii**.
2   A GOQ is one that is recognised by the Race Relations Act as being acceptable, e.g. an advert for a male secretary to work abroad in a country with different employment laws, and cases where for the sake of authenticity, e.g. in waiting or acting, someone from a particular racial group is required, e.g. Irish bar staff to work in Irish pub.

Equal Pay Act 1970

1   Pay, fringe benefits and sick pay.
2   She would be entitled to equal pay for work of equal value.

Employment Protection, Trade Union Reform and Employment Rights Act 1996

1   A contract of employment would contain – the names of employer and employee, date when employment starts, scale or rate of pay, when payment is made, hours, holiday pay, sick pay, entitlements to pension scheme, etc.
2   Employees have the right to an itemised pay slip setting out gross pay, deductions and net pay.
3   Fair dismissal could be for persistent bad timekeeping, wilful destruction of company property, or lack of qualifications and skills to do the job.
4   Seven days' notice.
5   Employers must recognise a trade union where at least 40 per cent of those eligible to do so take part in a ballot, and a majority of those voting are in favour of recognition. If over 50 per cent are already members of the union it should be recognised.
6   Risk assessment is an assessment of the risks and dangers involved with various activities and processes in the workplace.

Disability Discrimination Act 1995

1   Employers of more than 20 people must accommodate the needs of the disabled, and establish rights of access for the disabled.
2   Discrimination is defined as treating a disabled person less favourably than others would be treated (and the treatment is unjustified).

Working Time Regulations and Directive 1993

1   Working time is time when the worker is at the employer's disposal and carrying out their duties.
2   48 hours averaged over 17 weeks.
3   Yes they can opt out.
4   13 weeks' parental leave.

Glossary and further terms

Arbitrator – a person appointed to settle a dispute.

Articles of Association – a document setting out the details of the internal relationships that exist within the company, e.g. when company meetings will be held, how directors will be chosen, and so on.

Articles of the Treaty of Rome – the Articles of the Treaty of Rome which established the framework for the European Union have further been amended by the Single European Act in 1986, and in 1993 by the Maastricht Treaty. Further amendments were made in the Amsterdam Treaty of 1997 which has renumbered the various articles which contain the primary legislation. Examples which are relevant to business include:
* free movement of goods (Arts 30–31)
* agriculture (Arts 32–38)
* free movement of persons, services and capital (Arts 39–60)
* transport (Arts 70–90)
* common rules on competition and taxation (Arts 81–97)
* economic and monetary policy (Arts 98–124)
* employment (Arts 125–30)
* consumer protection (Art 153)
* environment (Arts 174–76)

Bailment – the transfer by one person to another of possession but not ownership of an asset.

Board of Directors – a body consisting of representatives of shareholders in a company with the responsibility for looking after the interests of shareholders.

Burden of proof – obligation to prove one's case.

Certificate of Incorporation – the document that certifies that a company has a company status, i.e. that it is recognised in law as being a body that can sue and be sued.

Civil law – law governing relationships between members of society but not including criminal offences. Including contract law and disputes between individuals and organisations.

Consideration compensation, payment or reward.

Contract of employment – legal document setting out terms and conditions of employment.

Creditors – individuals or other businesses that are owed money by a business.

Debtors – individuals or companies who owe money to the business.

Dividend – shareholders' share of profit made by a company.

Equity – a company's equity is its total capital value less all outside liabilities including those to holders of debentures and preferential shares but excepting those to ordinary shareholders. Ordinary shareholders are the owners of the company and hence its equity – which is why their shares are also known as 'equities'.

European Communities Act 1972 – in 1972 the UK became a full member of the European Community. The European Communities Act 1972 set out the principle that Community Law overrides English law where the latter is inconsistent with it. Section 3 of the Communities Act binds our courts to abide by Community law.

European Union – an economic, social and political union between major countries in Europe such as the UK, France and Germany.

Injunction – a judicial order restraining a person from an act or compelling redress to the injured party.

Invitation to treat – a situation in which an individual or business holds themselves open to offers without having yet made a final offer.

Judicial precedent – a judgment which provides the basis for future case law.

Limited liability – the limitation of what the owners of a company can be sued for – the top limit being the sum that they have invested in the business.

Liquidation – a process whereby a corporate body such as a company is dissolved by an administrator.

Negligence – lack of proper care and attention.

Nominal value – the face value of a share or other item.

Offer – a statement of the terms by which an offeror is prepared to be bound in agreeing to a contract.

Simple contract – a contract made orally or in writing but not in deed.

Single European Act 1986 – this set out to abolish all restraints to trade within the European Union by 1992.

Speciality contract – a contract made by deed.

Supreme Court – until recently, the House of Lords was the highest appeal court in the UK. However, in 2003 the government announced that the Law Lords would be replaced by a Supreme Court.

Third party – an intermediary involved in an agreement. For example, an agent employed by another (the principal) to put that other into contractual relationship with a third party.

Tort – breach of duty (other than under contract) leading to a claim for negligence.

Waive – refrain from using or insisting on using a claim, right etc.

Winding up – the liquidation or dissolution of a company.

Working Time Regulations – the Working Time Regulations implement the European Union's Working Time Directive, 1993. However, because the UK Conservative government did not sign the EU's Social Chapter of the Maastricht Treaty, this legislation only became applicable in the UK in 1998 (under Labour).

Index